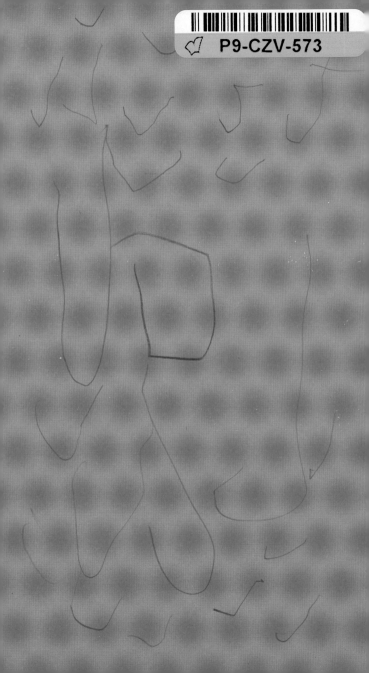

P9-CZV-573

to

from

on

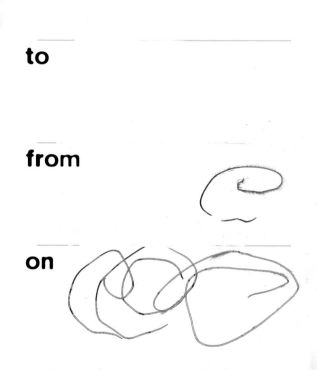

Remember your Creator in the
days of your youth.

Ecclesiastes 12:1

God's Words of Life for Teens
Copyright© 2000 by The Zondervan Corporation

ISBN 0-310-98075-5

Excerpts taken from: *Teen Devotional Bible; New International Version.* Copyright © 1999 by The Zondervan Corporation. All rights reserved.

All Scripture quotations, unless otherwise noted, are taken from the *Holy Bible: New International Version.*® Copyright © 1973, 1978, 1984, by International Bible Society. Used by permission of ZondervanPublishingHouse. All rights reserved.

The "NIV" and "New International Version" trademarks are registered in the United States Patent and Trademark Office by International Bible Society. Use of either trademark requires the permission of the International Bible Society.

All rights reserved. No part of this publication may be reproduced, stored in a retrieval system, or transmitted in any form or by any means—electronic, mechanical, photocopy, recording, or any other—except for brief quotations in printed reviews, without the prior permission of the publisher.

Requests for information should be addressed to:
    Inspirio, the Gift Group of Zondervan
    Grand Rapids, Michigan 49530

Senior Editor: Gwen Ellis
Project Editor: Sarah Hupp
Designer: Veldheer Creative Services
Production Editor: Molly Detweiler

Printed in China

01 02 03 04/HK/9 8

God's Words of Life for
TEENS

from the New International Version

inspirio

The gift group of Zondervan

God's Words of Life on

God's Words of Life on
ABILITIES AND TALENTS

The LORD bestows favor and honor; no good thing does he withhold from those whose walk is blameless.

Psalm 84:11

God's gifts and his call are irrevocable.

Romans 11:29

We have different gifts, according to the grace given us. If a man's gift is prophesying, let him use it in proportion to his faith. If it is serving, let him serve; if it is teaching, let him teach; if it is encouraging, let him encourage; if it is contributing to the needs of others, let him give generously; if it is leadership, let him govern diligently; if it is showing mercy, let him do it cheerfully.

Romans 12:6–8

The LORD gives strength to his people;
    the LORD blesses his people with peace.

Psalm 29:11

To the [one] who pleases him, God gives wisdom, knowledge and happiness.

Ecclesiastes 2:26

He gives wisdom to the wise and knowledge to the discerning.

Daniel 2:21

God's Words of Life on
ABILITIES AND TALENTS

A man going on a journey ... called his servants and entrusted his property to them. To one he gave five talents of money, to another two talents, and to another one talent, each according to his ability. Then he went on his journey. The man who had received the five talents went at once and put his money to work and gained five more. So also, the one with the two talents gained two more. But the man who had received the one talent went off, dug a hole in the ground and hid his master's money.

After a long time the master of those servants returned and settled accounts with them. The man who had received the five talents brought the other five. "Master," he said, "you entrusted me with five talents. See, I have gained five more." His master replied, "Well done, good and faithful servant! You have been faithful with a few things; I will put you in charge of many things. Come and share your master's happiness!"

The man with the two talents also came. "Master," he said, "you entrusted me with two talents; see, I have gained two more." His master replied, "Well done, good and faithful servant! You have been faithful with a few things; I will put you in charge of many things. Come and share your master's happiness!"

Then the man who had received the one talent came. "Master," he said, "I knew that you

God's Words of Life on
ABILITIES AND TALENTS

are a hard man, harvesting where you have not sown and gathering where you have not scattered seed. So I was afraid and went out and hid your talent in the ground. See, here is what belongs to you." His master replied, "You wicked, lazy servant! So you knew that I harvest where I have not sown and gather where I have not scattered seed? Well then, you should have put my money on deposit with the bankers, so that when I returned I would have received it back with interest. Take the talent from him and give it to the one who has the ten talents. For everyone who has will be given more, and he will have an abundance."

Matthew 25:14–29

It is the spirit in a man, the breath of the Almighty, that gives him understanding.

Job 32:8

Each [one] has his own gift from God; one has this gift, another has that.

1 Corinthians 7:7

God gave Solomon wisdom and very great insight, and a breadth of understanding as measureless as the sand on the seashore.

1 Kings 4:29

God's Words of Life on
ABILITIES AND TALENTS

There are different kinds of gifts, but the same Spirit ... Now to each one the manifestation of the Spirit is given for the common good. To one there is given through the Spirit the message of wisdom, to another the message of knowledge by means of the same Spirit, to another faith by the same Spirit, to another gifts of healing by that one Spirit, to another miraculous powers, to another prophecy, to another distinguishing between spirits, to another speaking in different kinds of tongues, and to still another the interpretation of tongues. All these are the work of one and the same Spirit, and he gives them to each one, just as he determines.

1 Corinthians 12:4, 7–11

Each one should use whatever gift he has received to serve others, faithfully administering God's grace in its various forms.

1 Peter 4:10

In him you have been enriched in every way— in all your speaking and in all your knowledge.

1 Corinthians 1:5

Since you are eager to have spiritual gifts, try to excel in gifts that build up the church.

1 Corinthians 14:12

God's Words of Life on
ABILITIES AND TALENTS

Never be lacking in zeal, but keep your spiritual fervor, serving the Lord.

Romans 12:11

Whatever you do, work at it with all your heart, as working for the Lord, not for men, since you know that you will receive an inheritance from the Lord as a reward. It is the Lord Christ you are serving.

Colossians 3:23–24

Skill will bring success.

Ecclesiastes 10:10

I have filled him with the Spirit of God, with skill, ability and knowledge in all kinds of crafts.

Exodus 31:3

Devotional Thought on
ABILITIES AND TALENTS

GOD DESERVES THE CREDIT

I really want to be a rapper. One Sunday morning I performed at my church. After the service, nearly everyone I knew told me I did a great job. Even people I had never seen congratulated me and told me it was awesome. I appreciated all the compliments, and I almost let their praise go to my head. But I tried to shake off the temptation of pride by acknowledging the truth: God has given me a talent, and all I can do is thank him for it. God hates selfish pride. He has given us everything. Without God we have nothing; we're completely helpless.

King David was a powerful guy, and he let it go to his head. He thought he could use his own power to do things. But once he remembered that God is in control of everything, David was like, "Whoa, what was I thinking?" He had let pride get the best of him.

Whenever I'm tempted to be proud and think I'm really talented, I need to remember that it's only because of God that I have any talent at all. He deserves all the credit for everything I do.

JOSH

God's Words of Life on
ACCEPTING OTHERS

Accept one another ... just as Christ accepted you, in order to bring praise to God.

Romans 15:7

If you show special attention to the man wearing fine clothes and say, "Here's a good seat for you," but say to the poor man, "You stand there" or "Sit on the floor by my feet," have you not discriminated among yourselves and become judges with evil thoughts?

James 2:3–4

Jesus said, "Do not judge, or you too will be judged. For in the same way you judge others, you will be judged, and with the measure you use, it will be measured to you."

Matthew 7:1–2

Accept him whose faith is weak, without passing judgment on disputable matters. One man's faith allows him to eat everything, but another man, whose faith is weak, eats only vegetables. The man who eats everything must not look down on him who does not, and the man who does not eat everything must not condemn the man who does, for God has accepted him. Who are you to judge someone else's servant? To his own master he stands or falls.

Romans 14:1–4

God's Words of Life on
ACCEPTING OTHERS

Let us stop passing judgment on one another.

Romans 14:13

If you show favoritism, you sin and are convicted by the law as lawbreakers.

James 2:9

Jesus said, "He who is least among you all—he is the greatest."

Luke 9:48

It is the Lord who judges me. Therefore judge nothing before the appointed time; wait till the Lord comes. He will bring to light what is hidden in darkness and will expose the motives of men's hearts. At that time each will receive his praise from God.

1 Corinthians 4:4–5

Judgment without mercy will be shown to anyone who has not been merciful. Mercy triumphs over judgment!

James 2:13

Defend the cause of the weak and fatherless;
    maintain the rights of the poor and
        oppressed.
Rescue the weak and needy;
    deliver them from the hand of the wicked.

Psalm 82:3–4

God's Words of Life on
ACCEPTING OTHERS

Stop judging by mere appearances, and make a right judgment.

John 7:24

To show partiality in judging is not good.

Proverbs 24:23

Jesus said, "Do to others as you would have them do to you."

Luke 6:31

Honor one another above yourselves.

Romans 12:10

There is neither Jew nor Greek, slave nor free, male nor female, for you are all one in Christ Jesus.

Galatians 3:28

No one has ever seen God; but if we love one another, God lives in us and his love is made complete in us.

1 John 4:12

UNFAIR JUDGES

A new kid came to our school last year, and he was a little on the heavy side. No one gave him a chance to show what kind of person he was; instead, everyone judged him by his weight. Unfortunately, I did too. Later in the year, many of us got to know him better, and he turned out to be really cool. I felt so guilty about the way we acted earlier, and I wish we hadn't judged him because of his appearance.

I'm sure everybody has treated someone unfairly at one time or another. And most of us can be kind of shallow and sometimes judge people by how they look. But God is never shallow. He cares about all of us—not because of what we look like, but because of who we are.

Flip through your school yearbook. Pay special attention to all the different kinds of people you see. God made each person unique. You can thank God for the unique way he's made you and for the way he's made other people too.

SPENCER

15

God's Words of Life on
ANGER

A gentle answer turns away wrath, but a harsh word stirs up anger.

Proverbs 15:1

An angry man stirs up dissension, and a hot-tempered one commits many sins.

Proverbs 29:22

Do not make friends with a hot-tempered man, do not associate with one easily angered, or you may learn his ways and get yourself ensnared.

Proverbs 22:24–25

Refrain from anger and turn from wrath; do not fret—it leads only to evil.

Psalm 37:8

Better a patient man than a warrior, a man who controls his temper than one who takes a city.

Proverbs 16:32

A patient man has great understanding, but a quick-tempered man displays folly.

Proverbs 14:29

Take note of this: Everyone should be quick to listen, slow to speak and slow to become angry, for man's anger does not bring about the righteous life that God desires.

James 1:19–20

Do not take revenge, my friends, but leave
room for God's wrath, for it is written: "It is
mine to avenge; I will repay," says the Lord.

Romans 12:19

If your enemy is hungry, give him food to eat;
if he is thirsty, give him water to drink.

Proverbs 25:21

Jesus said, "I tell you that anyone who is angry
with his brother will be subject to judgment."

Matthew 5:22

A wise man fears the LORD and shuns evil. A
fool is hotheaded and reckless. A quick-tempered man does foolish things.

Proverbs 14:16–17

A patient man calms a quarrel.

Proverbs 15:18

Starting a quarrel is like breaching a dam; so
drop the matter before a dispute breaks out.

Proverbs 17:14

I want men everywhere to lift up holy hands in
prayer, without anger or disputing.

1 Timothy 2:8

God's Words of Life on
ANGER

The LORD looked with favor on Abel and his offering, but on Cain and his offering he did not look with favor. So Cain was very angry, and his face was downcast. Then the LORD said to Cain, "Why are you angry? Why is your face downcast? If you do what is right, will you not be accepted? But if you do not do what is right, sin is crouching at your door; it desires to have you, but you must master it."

Genesis 4:4-7

[Love] is not easily angered, it keeps no record of wrongs.

1 Corinthians 13:5

The LORD is compassionate and gracious,
   slow to anger, abounding in love.
He will not always accuse,
   nor will he harbor his anger forever.

Psalm 103:8-9

Be completely humble and gentle; be patient, bearing with one another in love. Make every effort to keep the unity of the Spirit through the bond of peace.

Ephesians 4:2-3

Devotional Thought on
ANGER

DON'T GIVE IN TO ANGER!

We know what it's like to be wronged. We know how it feels when we find out someone has spread vicious rumors about us or dissed us to all our friends.

Anger is real. We all experience it. Because anger is such a strong emotion, it's easy to act on it with some kind of physical response. It happens all the time.

There's a better way. Trouble is, the better way is not always the easy way. Sometimes doing what's right is much harder than doing what's not right.

Take Jesus, for instance. He was betrayed by his friend and disciple, and he was being arrested for something he didn't do. Peter was ready to fight, but Jesus stopped him. What Jesus said was shocking. He said something like, "Hey, I could wipe these guys out with a whole truckload of angels, but I'm not going to fight these people. I am going to trust in the power of God instead of the power of violence." Wow! Jesus resisted using violence, and he can help us do the same.

God's Words of Life on
ATTITUDE

Your attitude should be the same as that of Christ Jesus. Who, being in very nature God, did not consider equality with God something to be grasped, but made himself nothing, taking the very nature of a servant being made in human likeness. And being found in appearance as a man, he humbled himself and became obedient to death—even death on a cross! Therefore God exalted him to the highest place and gave him the name that is above every name.

Philippians 2:5–9

The good man brings good things out of the good stored up in his heart, and the evil man brings evil things out of the evil stored up in his heart. For out of the overflow of his heart his mouth speaks.

Luke 6:45

Wait for the LORD
    and keep his way.
He will exalt you.

Psalm 37:34

Do everything without complaining or arguing, so that you may become blameless and pure, children of God without fault.

Philippians 2:14–15

God's Words of Life on
ATTITUDE

Let us ... make every effort to do what leads to peace.

Romans 14:19

What does the LORD require of you? To act justly and to love mercy and to walk humbly with your God.

Micah 6:8

You were taught ... to be made new in the attitude of your minds; and to put on the new self, created to be like God in true righteousness and holiness.

Ephesians 4:22–24

Speak to one another with psalms, hymns and spiritual songs. Sing and make music in your heart to the Lord.

Ephesians 5:19

Let the word of Christ dwell in you richly as you teach and admonish one another with all wisdom.

Colossians 3:16

Whoever claims to live in him must walk as Jesus did.

1 John 2:6

Above all else, guard your heart, for it is the wellspring of life.

Proverbs 4:23

God's Words of Life on
ATTITUDE

I try to please everybody in every way. For I am not seeking my own good but the good of many, so that they may be saved.

1 Corinthians 10:33

Jesus said, "Whoever wants to become great among you must be your servant, and whoever wants to be first must be your slave—just as the Son of Man did not come to be served, but to serve, and to give his life as a ransom for many."

Matthew 20:26–28

Be filled to the measure of all the fullness of God.

Ephesians 3:19

Nobody should seek his own good, but the good of others.

1 Corinthians 10:24

Each of us should please his neighbor for his good, to build him up.

Romans 15:2

The greatest among you will be your servant. For whoever exalts himself will be humbled, and whoever humbles himself will be exalted.

Matthew 23:11–12

Be kind and compassionate to one another, forgiving each other, just as in Christ God forgave you.

Ephesians 4:32

Devotional Thought on
ATTITUDE

A PIECE IN GOD'S PUZZLE

God's name is written all over us. That's a pretty radical statement. And it's important to understand what it means. It doesn't mean God makes us into religious zombies who walk around like robots and say "Hallelujah" all the time. And it doesn't mean we live perfect lives. No. God's name is written all over us in *the way we are made*—our gifts, our personalities, our strengths and weaknesses, our likes and dislikes, our desire to know God better. All those things come from God; all of them draw us closer. Everything about us is *at home* when we are with God. When we give ourselves to God, we are *coming home to God!* Since we *belong* to God, we never feel really whole or full or completed until we come back *to where we belong.* It is like we are the missing piece in a huge puzzle, and when we fit our unique shape into God's puzzle, the puzzle is complete.

Think back to the time you asked Jesus to come into your life. Then pray, "God, help me to see you in me. Help me to show others your name written all over me."

God's Words of Life on
BIBLE STUDY

Everything that was written in the past was written to teach us, so that through endurance and the encouragement of the Scriptures we might have hope.

Romans 15:4

The word of God is living and active. Sharper than any double-edged sword, it penetrates even to dividing soul and spirit, joints and marrow; it judges the thoughts and attitudes of the heart.

Hebrews 4:12

Like newborn babies, crave pure spiritual milk, so that by it you may grow up in your salvation.

1 Peter 2:2

Jesus said, "Take my yoke upon you and learn from me, for I am gentle and humble in heart, and you will find rest for your souls. For my yoke is easy and my burden is light."

Matthew 11:29–30

Oh, how I love your law!
   I meditate on it all day long.

Psalm 119:97

Let us discern for ourselves what is right; let us learn together what is good.

Job 34:4

God's Words of Life on
BIBLE STUDY

Grow in the grace and knowledge of our Lord
and Savior Jesus Christ. To him be glory both
now and forever!

2 Peter 3:18

My purpose is that they may be encouraged in
heart and united in love, so that they may have
the full riches of complete understanding, in
order that they may know the mystery of God,
namely, Christ, in whom are hidden all the
treasures of wisdom and knowledge.

Colossians 2:2–3

This is my prayer: that your love may abound
more and more in knowledge and depth of
insight, so that you may be able to discern
what is best and may be pure and blameless
until the day of Christ.

Philippians 1:9–10

Your statutes are my heritage forever.

Psalm 119:111

You must understand that no prophecy of
Scripture came about by the prophet's own
interpretation. For prophecy never had its origin
in the will of man, but men spoke from God as
they were carried along by the Holy Spirit.

2 Peter 1:20–21

God's Words of Life on
BIBLE STUDY

I have more insight than all my teachers,
    for I meditate on your statutes.
I have more understanding than the elders,
    for I obey your precepts.
I have kept my feet from every evil path
    so that I might obey your word.
I have not departed from your laws,
    for you yourself have taught me.
How sweet are your words to my taste,
    sweeter than honey to my mouth!
I gain understanding from your precepts;
    therefore I hate every wrong path.

Psalm 119:99–104

Your hands made me and formed me; give me understanding to learn your commands.

Psalm 119:73

Come near to God and he will come near to you.

James 4:8

The grass withers and the flowers fall, but the word of our God stands forever.

Isaiah 40:8

All Scripture is God-breathed and is useful for teaching, rebuking, correcting and training in righteousness, so that the man of God may be thoroughly equipped for every good work.

2 Timothy 3:16–17

God's Words of Life on
BIBLE STUDY

The law of the LORD is perfect
    reviving the soul.
The statutes of the LORD are trustworthy,
    making wise the simple.
The precepts of the LORD are right,
    giving joy to the heart.
The commands of the LORD are radiant,
    giving light to the eyes.
The fear of the LORD is pure,
    enduring forever.
The ordinances of the LORD are sure
    and altogether righteous.
They are more precious than gold,
    than much pure gold;
they are sweeter than honey,
    than honey from the comb.
By them is your servant warned;
    in keeping them there is great reward.

Psalm 19:7–11

I remember your ancient laws, O LORD,
    and I find comfort in them.

Psalm 119:52

Your word, O LORD, is eternal
    it stands firm in the heavens.

Psalm 119:89

Every word of God is flawless; he is a shield to
those who take refuge in him.

Proverbs 30:5

God's Words of Life on
BIBLE STUDY

Do not let this Book of the Law depart from your mouth; meditate on it day and night, so that you may be careful to do everything written in it. Then you will be prosperous and successful.

Joshua 1:8

When your words came, I ate them; they were my joy and my heart's delight, for I bear your name, O Lord God Almighty.

Jeremiah 15:16

How can a young man keep his way pure?
    By living according to your word.

Psalm 119:9

"As the rain and the snow
    come down from heaven,
and do not return to it
    without watering the earth
and making it bud and flourish,
    so that it yields seed for the sower and
        bread for the eater,
so is my word that goes out from my mouth:
    It will not return to me empty,
but will accomplish what I desire
    and achieve the purpose for which I sent
        it," says the Lord.

Isaiah 55:10–11

Devotional Thought on
BIBLE STUDY

THE BEST KIND OF STUDYING

If you're a Christian, it makes sense that you'd want to learn as much as you could about Jesus Christ and his Word. You can do that by talking about the Bible with your friends and family, writing down verses or memorizing them. You can also learn by going to church and listening to what your pastor or youth leader says.

Think about it—of all the things you learn in your life, what's the most important? It's not algebra or biology! Although studying these subjects is important and necessary, the most important thing is to know who God is and what he wants you to do in your life. And the more you learn about him, the more you feel secure and have strength for whatever challenges you have to face. Reading the Bible is the best kind of studying!

KELLI

God's Words of Life on
DATING

He who walks with the wise grows wise.

Proverbs 13:20

Treat younger men as brothers, older women as mothers, and younger women as sisters, with absolute purity.

1 Timothy 5:1–2

The LORD does not look at the things man looks at. Man looks at the outward appearance, but the LORD looks at the heart.

1 Samuel 16:7

Guard yourself in your spirit.

Malachi 2:15

Do not . . . awaken love until it so desires.

Song of Songs 2:7

I would like you to be free from concern. An unmarried man is concerned about the Lord's affairs—how he can please the Lord . . . An unmarried woman or virgin is concerned about the Lord's affairs: Her aim is to be devoted to the Lord in both body and spirit. I am saying this for your own good, not to restrict you, but that you may live in a right way in undivided devotion to the Lord.

1 Corinthians 7:32,34–35

God's Words of Life on
DATING

Pursue righteousness, faith, love and peace, along with those who call on the Lord out of a pure heart.

2 Timothy 2:22

As God's chosen people, holy and dearly loved, clothe yourselves with compassion, kindness, humility, gentleness and patience.

Colossians 3:12

All of you, live in harmony with one another; be sympathetic, love as brothers, be compassionate and humble.

1 Peter 3:8

Love is patient, love is kind. It does not envy, it does not boast, it is not proud. It is not rude, it is not self-seeking, it is not easily angered, it keeps no record of wrongs. Love does not delight in evil but rejoices with the truth. It always protects, always trusts, always hopes, always perseveres.

1 Corinthians 13:4–7

Your beauty should not come from outward adornment, such as braided hair and the wearing of gold jewelry and fine clothes. Instead, it should be that of your inner self, the unfading beauty of a gentle and quiet spirit, which is of great worth in God's sight.

1 Peter 3:3–4

God's Words of Life on
DATING

Whatever is true, whatever is noble, whatever is right, whatever is pure, whatever is lovely, whatever is admirable—if anything is excellent or praiseworthy—think about such things.

Philippians 4:8

Blessed are the pure in heart, for they will see God.

Matthew 5:8

Each of you should learn to control his own body in a way that is holy and honorable.

1 Thessalonians 4:4

Show proper respect to everyone.

1 Peter 2:17

Be kind and compassionate to one another. ... Be imitators of God, therefore, as dearly loved children and live a life of love, just as Christ loved us and gave himself up for us as a fragrant offering and sacrifice to God.

Ephesians 4:32—5:1-2

THE BEST TIME

Recently this boy asked me to be his girl-friend. I told him no, because I think I'm too young to get into that kind of thing. And my mom doesn't want me to date until I'm sixteen anyway. I knew it just wasn't the right time.

It's important to realize that love isn't something to play around with. Song of Songs makes that clear when it says, "Do not arouse or awaken love until it so desires" (Song of Songs 2:7). We shouldn't run into a dating relationship simply because everyone else thinks it's OK. God wants us to wait for the right person, not because he doesn't want us to have a good time but because he wants us to have the *best* time.

Because God cares about us so deeply, he wants us to save romantic love for a relationship he would be proud of. We don't know when or if that will happen, but we can trust God to take care of us in his way and in his time.

ROBYN

God's Words of Life on
DECISIONS

The heart of the discerning acquires knowledge; the ears of the wise seek it out.

Proverbs 18:15

If any of you lacks wisdom, he should ask God, who gives generously to all without finding fault, and it will be given to him.

James 1:5

The way of a fool seems right to him, but a wise man listens to advice.

Proverbs 12:15

Guide me in your truth and teach me,
for you are God my Savior,
and my hope is in you all day long.

Psalm 25:5

Help us, O God our Savior,
for the glory of your name.

Psalm 79:9

Trust in the LORD with all your heart and lean
not on your own understanding;
in all your ways acknowledge him, and he will
make your paths straight.

Proverbs 3:5–6

God's Words of Life on
DECISIONS

You know his will and approve of what is
superior because you are instructed by the law.

Romans 2:18

The LORD confides in those who fear him;
    he makes his covenant known to them.

Psalm 25:14

It is God who works in you to will and to act
according to his good purpose.

Philippians 2:13

You have known the holy Scriptures, which are
able to make you wise.

2 Timothy 3:15

Buy the truth and do not sell it; get wisdom,
discipline and understanding.

Proverbs 23:23

The discerning heart seeks knowledge.

Proverbs 15:14

Make plans by seeking advice; ... obtain
guidance.

Proverbs 20:18

Direct me in the path of your commands,
    for there I find delight.

Psalm 119:35

God's Words of Life on
DECISIONS

Direct my footsteps according to your word.

Psalm 119:133

The Spirit of truth ... will guide you into all truth. He will not speak on his own; he will speak only what he hears, and he will tell you what is yet to come.

John 16:13

The LORD will guide you always.

Isaiah 58:11

"I guide you in the way of wisdom and lead you along straight paths," says the LORD.

Proverbs 4:11

Teach me to do your will,
    for you are my God;
may your good Spirit
    lead me on level ground.

Psalm 143:10

Since you are my rock and my fortress,
    for the sake of your name lead and guide me.

Psalm 31:3

In your unfailing love you will lead the people you have redeemed.

Exodus 15:13

God's Words of Life on
DECISIONS

Jesus said, "Do not let your hearts be troubled. Trust in God; trust also in me."

John 14:1

Let him who walks in the dark, who has no light, trust in the name of the LORD and rely on his God.

Isaiah 50:10

Commit your way to the LORD;
    trust in him and he will do this:
He will make your righteousness shine like the
        dawn,
    the justice of your cause like the noonday sun.

Psalm 37:5–6

Teach me your way, O LORD.

Psalm 27:11

In his heart a man plans his course, but the LORD determines his steps.

Proverbs 16:9

"Counsel and sound judgment are mine; I have understanding and power," says the LORD. "I love those who love me, and those who seek me find me."

Proverbs 8:14, 17

God's Words of Life on
DECISIONS

"I will instruct you and teach you in the way you should go; I will counsel you and watch over you," says the LORD.

Psalm 32:8

Listen to advice and accept instruction, and in the end you will be wise.

Proverbs 19:20

May the Lord direct your hearts into God's love and Christ's perseverance.

2 Thessalonians 3:5

Keep your father's commands and do not forsake your mother's teaching. Bind them upon your heart forever; fasten them around your neck. When you walk, they will guide you; when you sleep, they will watch over you; when you awake, they will speak to you.

Proverbs 6:20–22

Devotional Thought on
DECISIONS

MAKING TOUGH DECISIONS

Have you ever been lost? Maybe you got on the wrong trail on a youth group hike or maybe you just lost your mom in the store when you were little. You were stuck. You had no idea where to go.

Sometimes we face situations like that in other areas of life. Maybe you're trying to decide which parent to live with this year. Or you might be thinking about changing classes because you don't get along with your teacher. Or maybe a friend is begging you to do something you don't really want to do. Whatever the decision, you don't know which direction to go. And you're afraid that you might choose the wrong direction, so you don't choose anything at all.

When we face tough decisions about which direction to go, it's not always obvious to us which road to take. The Bible tells us to ask God to give us wisdom. It doesn't say that God will tell us *exactly* what to do; instead it says that God gives us the *wisdom* to decide.

What decision are you facing right now? Spend a few moments in prayer asking God for wisdom to help you make a good decision. Then thank him in advance for taking care of you.

God's Words of Life on
DOUBT

God has said, "Never will I leave you; never will I forsake you." So we say with confidence, "The Lord is my helper; I will not be afraid."

Hebrews 13:5–6

Jesus said, "If anyone says to this mountain, 'Go, throw yourself into the sea,' and does not doubt in his heart but believes that what he says will happen, it will be done for him."

Mark 11:23

Against all hope, Abraham in hope believed and so became the father of many nations, just as it had been said to him, "So shall your off-spring be." ... He did not waver through unbelief regarding the promise of God, but was strengthened in his faith and gave glory to God, being fully persuaded that God had power to do what he had promised. This is why "it was credited to him as righteousness."

Romans 4:18, 20–22

Let him who walks in the dark, who has no light, trust in the name of the LORD and rely on his God.

Isaiah 50:10

Put your hope in the LORD
both now and forevermore.

Psalm 131:3

God's Words of Life on
DOUBT

Let us hold unswervingly to the hope we profess, for he who promised is faithful.

Hebrews 10:23

Jesus told him, "Because you have seen me, you have believed; blessed are those who have not seen and yet have believed."

John 20:29

Having believed, you were marked in him with a seal, the promised Holy Spirit, who is a deposit guaranteeing our inheritance until the redemption of those who are God's possession—to the praise of his glory.

Ephesians 1:13–14

I make known the end from the beginning, from ancient times, what is still to come. I say: My purpose will stand, and I will do all that I please. ... What I have said, that will I bring about; what I have planned, that will I do.

Isaiah 46:10–11

The one who calls you is faithful.

1 Thessalonians 5:24

Surely the arm of the LORD is not too short to save, nor his ear too dull to hear.

Isaiah 59:1

God's Words of Life on
DOUBT

Do not forget this one thing, dear friends: With the Lord a day is like a thousand years, and a thousand years are like a day. The Lord is not slow in keeping his promise, as some understand slowness. He is patient with you, not wanting anyone to perish, but everyone to come to repentance.

2 Peter 3:8–9

The peace of God, which transcends all understanding, will guard your hearts and your minds in Christ Jesus.

Philippians 4:7

Faith is being sure of what we hope for and certain of what we do not see.

Hebrews 11:1

This is the confidence we have in approaching God: that if we ask anything according to his will, he hears us. And if we know that he hears us—whatever we ask—we know that we have what we asked of him.

1 John 5:14–15

REAL DOUBTS

When you doubt, take heart. You're in good company. When Thomas doubted the resurrection, Jesus gave him proof (John 20:27). When a doubting man asked for a miracle, Jesus helped him (Mark 9:17–27). In fact, the Bible commands us to be merciful to those who doubt (Jude 22).

Sometimes terrible tragedies cause us to doubt God's goodness or fairness. The best medicine in this case is prayer and patience. Just tell God how you feel and wait for him to remind you of his kindness and love. If you doubt the basic truth of God or his Word, talk to your pastor or your parents. There are very good reasons why we believe.

Sometimes we doubt our own faith. We wonder if we really belong to God. In this case, pop some promise pills. John 6:37 says Jesus will never drive away those who come to him. John 10:28 says no one can snatch God's people from his hand. Romans 8:38–39 says nothing can separate us from God's love. Thankfully, salvation does not rest on the strength of your faith but on the power of God's promises. Take that medicine, and you'll start feeling much better!

God's Words of Life on
DRUGS AND ALCOHOL

The kingdom of God is not a matter of eating and drinking, but of righteousness, peace and joy in the Holy Spirit, because anyone who serves Christ in this way is pleasing to God and approved by men. Let us therefore make every effort to do what leads to peace and to mutual edification.

Romans 14:17–19

Do not get drunk on wine ... Instead, be filled with the Spirit.

Ephesians 5:18

Those who get drunk, get drunk at night. But since we belong to the day, let us be self-controlled.

1 Thessalonians 5:7–8

Woe to those who rise early in the morning to run after their drinks, who stay up late at night till they are inflamed with wine. They have no regard for the deeds of the LORD, no respect for the work of his hands.

Isaiah 5:11–12

Do not gaze at wine when it is red, when it sparkles in the cup, when it goes down smoothly! In the end it bites like a snake and poisons like a viper. Your eyes will see strange sights and your mind imagine confusing things.

Proverbs 23:31–33

Devotional Thought on
DRUGS AND ALCOHOL

LEGALISM OR LIBERTY?

Television, alcohol, clothing styles—how do you know what to do in these areas? There are two extremes to avoid. The first one is *license*—that's the party-on attitude that says, "Hey, if it's not illegal, it's fine." Christians get into all kinds of trouble if their standards aren't higher than this.

The other extreme is just as dangerous. It's called *legalism,* which is thinking that you have to obey a huge list of do's and don'ts in order to be close to God.

Between these two extremes is real *liberty,* the ability to enjoy what's good in life while avoiding what's bad. Here are 4 questions to ask when you encounter a gray area:

(1)   Will it please God? Avoid anything that God will eventually judge and destroy.
(2)   Will it help me? Think about whether the activity is beneficial for your health and spiritual growth.
(3)   Could it enslave me? If the activity is tempting, addicting or really time-consuming, watch out.
(4)   Will it hurt someone else? How would it feel to be in their shoes?

Put your questionable activities to these tests, and you're likely to find your way through life's gray areas.

God's Words of Life on
EMBARRASSMENT

Because the Sovereign LORD helps me, I will not be disgraced. Therefore have I set my face like flint, and I know I will not be put to shame.

Isaiah 50:7

Do not be ashamed to testify about our Lord.

2 Timothy 1:8

There is now no condemnation for those who are in Christ Jesus.

Romans 8:1

If you suffer as a Christian, do not be ashamed, but praise God that you bear that name.

1 Peter 4:16

I am not ashamed of the gospel, because it is the power of God for the salvation of everyone who believes: first for the Jew, then for the Gentile.

Romans 1:16

The LORD is my light and my salvation—
  whom shall I fear?
The LORD is the stronghold of my life—
  of whom shall I be afraid?

Psalm 27:1

For Christ's sake, I delight in weaknesses, in insults, in hardships, in persecutions, in difficulties. For when I am weak, then I am strong.

2 Corinthians 12:10

God's Words of Life on
EMBARRASSMENT

For it is with your heart that you believe and
are justified, and it is with your mouth that
you confess and are saved. As the Scripture
says, "Anyone who trusts in Jesus will never be
put to shame."

Romans 10:10–11

Instead of their shame my people will receive a
double portion, and instead of disgrace they
will rejoice in their inheritance; and so they
will inherit a double portion in their land, and
everlasting joy will be theirs.

Isaiah 61:7

Do not be afraid; you will not suffer shame. Do
not fear disgrace; you will not be humiliated.
You will forget the shame of your youth.

Isaiah 54:4

In you, O LORD, I have taken refuge;
    let me never be put to shame.

Psalm 71:1

By faith Moses, when he had grown up,
refused to be known as the son of Pharaoh's
daughter. He chose to be mistreated along with
the people of God rather than to enjoy the
pleasures of sin for a short time. He regarded
disgrace for the sake of Christ as of greater
value than the treasures of Egypt, because he
was looking ahead to his reward.

Hebrews 11:24–26

God's Words of Life on
EMBARRASSMENT

It is better, if it is God's will, to suffer for doing good than for doing evil.

1 Peter 3:17

I am not ashamed, because I know whom I have believed, and am convinced that God is able to guard what I have entrusted to him for that day.

2 Timothy 1:12

In Scripture it says: "See, I lay a stone in Zion, a chosen and precious cornerstone, and the one who trusts in him will never be put to shame."

1 Peter 2:6

Let us fix our eyes on Jesus, the author and perfecter of our faith, who for the joy set before him endured the cross, scorning its shame, and sat down at the right hand of the throne of God. Consider him who endured such opposition from sinful men, so that you will not grow weary and lose heart.

Hebrews 12:2–3

Devotional Thought on
EMBARRASSMENT

WHAT WOULD *YOU* DO?

Like a lot of people, I sometimes wear stuff to school that shows I'm a Christian. It helps me think about the things I do and say. But deep inside, I'm scared someone will ask me what it means or make fun of me for wearing it. I have to admit, sometimes I'm embarrassed about my faith.

When I read verses like Jeremiah 20:8-11, it helps me remember that I'm not the first person to worry about what other people will think if I talk about my faith. These verses also help me remember that God gave me a job to do—to tell people about him. I could be the only Christian another person meets. I could be their only chance to find out about Jesus. If I keep quiet because I'm afraid that person will make fun of me, I'm not doing what God wants me to do.

JAKE

God's Words of Life on
EMOTIONS

Above all else, guard your heart, for it is the wellspring of life.

Proverbs 4:23

The mind controlled by the Spirit is life and peace.

Romans 8:6

Do not conform any longer to the pattern of this world, but be transformed by the renewing of your mind.

Romans 12:2

I will give you a new heart and put a new spirit in you; I will remove from you your heart of stone and give you a heart of flesh. And I will put my Spirit in you and move you to follow my decrees and be careful to keep my laws.

Ezekiel 36:26–27

Be wise, and keep your heart on the right path.

Proverbs 23:19

Search me, O God, and know my heart;
    test me and know my anxious thoughts.

Psalm 139:23

Preserve sound judgment and discernment, do not let them out of your sight.

Proverbs 3:21

God's Words of Life on
EMOTIONS

How long must I wrestle with my thoughts
    and every day have sorrow in my heart? ...
Look on me and answer, O Lord my God.
    Give light to my eyes ...
I trust in your unfailing love;
    my heart rejoices in your salvation.
I will sing to the Lord,
    for he has been good to me.

Psalm 13:2–3, 5–6

I will praise the Lord, who counsels me;
    even at night my heart instructs me.
I have set the Lord always before me.
    Because he is at my right hand,
    I will not be shaken.
Therefore my heart is glad and my tongue
      rejoices;
    my body also will rest secure.

Psalm 16:7–9

May the words of my mouth and the medita-
      tion of my heart
    be pleasing in your sight,
O Lord, my Rock and my Redeemer.

Psalm 19:14

All my longings lie open before you, O Lord;
    my sighing is not hidden from you....
Come quickly to help me,
    O Lord my Savior.

Psalm 38:9, 22

God's Words of Life on
EMOTIONS

Grace, mercy and peace from God the Father and from Jesus Christ, the Father's Son, will be with us in truth and love.

2 John 1:3

Our mouths were filled with laughter,
　　our tongues with songs of joy . . . .
The LORD has done great things for us,
　　and we are filled with joy.

Psalm 126:2–3

Is anyone happy? Let him sing songs of praise.

James 5:13

Be happy, young man, while you are young,
　　and let your heart give you joy in the days
　　　of your youth.

Ecclesiastes 11:9

A happy heart makes the face cheerful.

Proverbs 15:13

May the righteous be glad
　　and rejoice before God;
　　　may they be happy and joyful.
Sing to God, sing praise to his name,
　　extol him who rides on the clouds—
　　　his name is the LORD—
　　and rejoice before him.

Psalm 68:3–4

Devotional Thought on
EMOTIONS

HANDLING YOUR EMOTIONS

When you step into your teenage years, God gives your growing body the gift of big emotions. You gain access to adult emotions that you've never felt before, and these emotions are turbo-charged! When you feel love, it can knock you down! When you get mad, you feel like knocking someone else down. These grown-up emotions can take over and control you if you're not careful.

So, what can you do? Here are some hints to help you get a grip on your emotions:

God understands your emotions. Not only did he *create* your emotions, Jesus came to earth, lived a human life and knows what it's like to *feel* strong emotions.

Feelings can fool you. Feelings can be so intense that they can cause you to do things you know aren't right. Anger, depression and jealousy can hurt you and others. If you give them control, they can make life tough.

Act on faith, not on feelings. Do what God wants you to do, in spite of your emotions. Don't worry—your feelings will follow. If you act on faith with your emotions, God can help you control all those up-and-down feelings.

God's Words of Life on
ENCOURAGEMENT

Cast your cares on the LORD
    and he will sustain you;
he will never let the righteous fall.

Psalm 55:22

Do not be anxious about anything.

Philippians 4:6

In my alarm I said,
    "I am cut off from your sight!"
Yet you heard my cry for mercy
    when I called to you for help ...
Be strong and take heart,
    all you who hope in the LORD.

Psalm 31:22, 24

My soul is downcast within me.
Yet this I call to mind
    and therefore I have hope:
Because of the LORD's great love we
        are not consumed,
    for his compassions never fail.
They are new every morning;
    great is your faithfulness.

Lamentations 3:20–23

Why are you downcast, O my soul?
    Why so disturbed within me?
Put your hope in God,
    for I will yet praise him,
    my Savior and my God.

Psalm 42:5–6

God's Words of Life on
ENCOURAGEMENT

Let the morning bring me word of your
          unfailing love,
     for I have put my trust in you.
Show me the way I should go,
     for to you I lift up my soul.

Psalm 143:8

The LORD is a refuge for the oppressed,
     a stronghold in times of trouble.

Psalm 9:9

You are my hiding place; you will protect me
from trouble and surround me with songs of
deliverance.

Psalm 32:7

The eternal God is your refuge, and underneath
are the everlasting arms.

Deuteronomy 33:27

God is our refuge and strength,
     an ever-present help in trouble.
Therefore we will not fear, though the earth
          give way
     and the mountains fall into the heart of
          the sea
     though its waters roar and foam
and the mountains quake with their surging.

Psalm 46:1–3

God's Words of Life on
ENCOURAGEMENT

My soul finds rest in God alone;
  my salvation comes from him.
He alone is my rock and my salvation;
  he is my fortress, I will never be shaken.

Psalm 62:1–2

My flesh and my heart may fail,
  but God is the strength of my heart
and my portion forever.

Psalm 73:26

When I said, "My foot is slipping,"
  your love, O LORD, supported me.
When anxiety was great within me,
  your consolation brought joy to my soul.

Psalm 94:18–19

He gives strength to the weary and increases
the power of the weak. Even youths grow tired
and weary, and young men stumble and fall;
but those who hope in the LORD will renew
their strength. They will soar on wings like
eagles; they will run and not grow weary, they
will walk and not be faint.

Isaiah 40:29–31

I am the LORD, your God, who takes hold of
your right hand and says to you, Do not fear; I
will help you.

Isaiah 41:13

God's Words of Life on
ENCOURAGEMENT

I sought the LORD, and he answered me;
  he delivered me from all my fears.

Psalm 34:4

When you pass through the waters, I will be
with you; and when you pass through the
rivers, they will not sweep over you. When you
walk through the fire, you will not be burned;
the flames will not set you ablaze.

Isaiah 43:2

In all their distress [the Savior] too was distressed,
and the angel of his presence saved them. In his
love and mercy he redeemed them; he lifted them
up and carried them all the days of old.

Isaiah 63:9

He will show compassion, so great is his
unfailing love.

Lamentations 3:32

Jesus said, "Come to me, all you who are
weary and burdened, and I will give you rest.
Take my yoke upon you and learn from me, for
I am gentle and humble in heart, and you will
find rest for your souls."

Matthew 11:28-29

I will refresh the weary and satisfy the faint.

Jeremiah 31:25

God's Words of Life on
ENCOURAGEMENT

The LORD upholds all those who
fall and lifts up all who are bowed down.

Psalm 145:14

Peace I leave with you; my peace I give you.

John 14:27

My grace is sufficient for you, for my power is
made perfect in weakness.

2 Corinthians 12:9

Though I have fallen, I will rise. Though I sit in
darkness, the LORD will be my light.

Micah 7:8

God, who has called you into fellowship with
his Son Jesus Christ our Lord, is faithful.

1 Corinthians 1:9

The LORD is good to those whose hope is in
him, to the one who seeks him.

Lamentations 3:25

Cast all your anxiety on him because he cares
for you.

1 Peter 5:7

Devotional Thought on
ENCOURAGEMENT

THE TOUGH TIMES

My life hasn't been easy. One of my parents died, and I have had a lot of bad days since then. People try to help me feel better, but it doesn't always work. Sometimes I feel completely alone, with no one to talk to. But even in those bad times, I know God is there for me.

I guess it's normal to get down sometimes. And it's normal to feel like your life is a big mess, especially when something awful happens. That's why God wants us to know we can count on him even when it seems like the whole world is against us.

No matter how down we feel, no matter how bad life seems, God is there. He has seen me through some really tough times, and I know he will do the same for anyone who asks for his help.

BRIAN

God's Words of Life on
FAITH IN GOD

Faith is being sure of what we hope for and certain of what we do not see.

Hebrews 11:1

By faith Noah, when warned about things not yet seen, in holy fear built an ark to save his family. By his faith he condemned the world and became heir of the righteousness that comes by faith.

Hebrews 11:7

Faith comes from hearing the message, and the message is heard through the word of Christ.

Romans 10:17

Without faith it is impossible to please God, because anyone who comes to him must believe that he exists and that he rewards those who earnestly seek him.

Hebrews 11:6

"Have faith in God," Jesus answered. "I tell you the truth, if anyone says to this mountain, 'Go, throw yourself into the sea,' and does not doubt in his heart but believes that what he says will happen, it will be done for him. Therefore I tell you, whatever you ask for in prayer, believe that you have received it, and it will be yours."

Mark 11:22-24

God's Words of Life on
FAITH IN GOD

By faith we understand that the universe was formed at God's command, so that what is seen was not made out of what was visible.

Hebrews 11:3

In the gospel a righteousness from God is revealed, a righteousness that is by faith from first to last, just as it is written: "The righteous will live by faith."

Romans 1:17

I do not have time to tell about Gideon, Barak, Samson, Jephthah, David, Samuel and the prophets, who through faith conquered kingdoms, administered justice, and gained what was promised; who shut the mouths of lions, quenched the fury of the flames, and escaped the edge of the sword; whose weakness was turned to strength; and who became powerful in battle and routed foreign armies. Women received back their dead, raised to life again. Others were tortured and refused to be released, so that they might gain a better resurrection. Some faced jeers and flogging, while still others were chained and put in prison. . . .the world was not worthy of them.

Hebrews 11:32–36, 38

God's Words of Life on
FAITH IN GOD

These [trials] have come so that your faith—of greater worth than gold, which perishes even though refined by fire—may be proved genuine and may result in praise, glory and honor when Jesus Christ is revealed. Though you have not seen him, you love him; and even though you do not see him now, you believe in him and are filled with an inexpressible and glorious joy, for you are receiving the goal of your faith, the salvation of your souls.

1 Peter 1:7–9

We live by faith, not by sight.

2 Corinthians 5:7

Pursue righteousness, faith, love and peace, along with those who call on the Lord out of a pure heart.

2 Timothy 2:22

Let us fix our eyes on Jesus, the author and perfecter of our faith, who for the joy set before him endured the cross, scorning its shame, and sat down at the right hand of the throne of God.

Hebrews 12:2

Abram believed the LORD, and he credited it to him as righteousness.

Genesis 15:6

God's Words of Life on
FAITH IN GOD

By faith Abraham, when called to go to a place he would later receive as his inheritance, obeyed and went, even though he did not know where he was going. By faith he made his home in the promised land like a stranger in a foreign country; he lived in tents, as did Isaac and Jacob, who were heirs with him of the same promise. For he was looking forward to the city with foundations, whose architect and builder is God.

By faith Abraham, even though he was past age—and Sarah herself was barren—was enabled to become a father because he considered him faithful who had made the promise. And so from this one man ... came descendants as numerous as the stars in the sky and as countless as the sand on the seashore.

Hebrews 11:8–12

I pray that you may be active in sharing your faith, so that you will have a full understanding of every good thing we have in Christ.

Philemon 1:6

Take up the shield of faith, with which you can extinguish all the flaming arrows of the evil one.

Ephesians 6:16

God's Words of Life on
FAITH IN GOD

By faith Moses' parents hid him for three months after he was born, because they saw he was no ordinary child, and they were not afraid of the king's edict.

By faith Moses, when he had grown up, refused to be known as the son of Pharaoh's daughter. He chose to be mistreated along with the people of God rather than to enjoy the pleasures of sin for a short time. He regarded disgrace for the sake of Christ as of greater value than the treasures of Egypt, because he was looking ahead to his reward. By faith he left Egypt, not fearing the king's anger; he persevered because he saw him who is invisible.

Hebrews 11:23–27

I have fought the good fight, I have finished the race, I have kept the faith. Now there is in store for me the crown of righteousness, which the Lord, the righteous Judge, will award to me on that day—and not only to me, but also to all who have longed for his appearing.

2 Timothy 4:7

So then, just as you received Christ Jesus as Lord, continue to live in him, rooted and built up in him, strengthened in the faith as you were taught, and overflowing with thankfulness.

Colossians 2:6–7

God's Words of Life on
FAITH IN GOD

We always thank God, the Father of our Lord Jesus Christ, when we pray for you, because we have heard of your faith in Christ Jesus and of the love you have for all the saints—the faith and love that spring from the hope that is stored up for you in heaven and that you have already heard about in the word of truth, the gospel that has come to you.

Colossians 1:3-6

In Christ and through faith in Christ we may approach God with freedom and confidence.

Ephesians 3:12

For it is by grace you have been saved, through faith—and this not from yourselves, it is the gift of God—not by works, so that no one can boast.

Ephesians 2:8-9

Everyone born of God overcomes the world. This is the victory that has overcome the world, even our faith.

1 John 5:4

The prayer offered in faith will make the sick person well; the Lord will raise him up.

James 5:15

God's Words of Life on
FAITH IN GOD

Remember your leaders, who spoke the word of God to you. Consider the outcome of their way of life and imitate their faith.

Hebrews 13:7

Let us draw near to God with a sincere heart in full assurance of faith.

Hebrews 10:22

Fight the good fight of the faith.

1 Timothy 6:12

Have faith in the Lord your God and you will be upheld.

2 Chronicles 20:20

Through Christ you believe in God, who raised him from the dead and glorified him, and so your faith and hope are in God.

1 Peter 1:21

Since we have been justified through faith, we have peace with God through our Lord Jesus Christ.

Romans 5:1

KEEP ON BELIEVING

You can't earn salvation. You can't earn God's love. It's not for sale. It's a gift he wants to give you. And it's a gift you accept through faith, and faith alone.

Jesus says, "I stand at the door and knock. If anyone hears my voice and opens the door, I will come in and eat with him, and he with me" (Revelation 3:20). Ask yourself, "Have I opened the door and invited Jesus into my life?" He promises that if you invite him in, he will come in. And if you've taken that step, you can know that you're saved.

People sometimes get confused because they base their faith on their feelings. Things can make you feel bad, but these things have nothing to do with whether or not you are a Christian. Even if you don't "feel" it, you can be sure you're a Christian because of the promises of Scripture.

Jesus says no one can snatch us out of his hand (John 10:27–29). We are in Jesus' grip of love and faithfulness, and his grip is so strong, nothing can pull us out of it.

So keep believing. God keeps his promises.

DAWSON MCALLISTER

God's Words of Life on
FAMILY RELATIONSHIPS

Children, obey your parents in the Lord, for this is right. "Honor your father and mother"—which is the first commandment with a promise—"that it may go well with you and that you may enjoy long life on the earth."

Ephesians 6:1–3

Both the one who makes men holy and those who are made holy are of the same family. So Jesus is not ashamed to call them brothers.

Hebrews 2:11

If anyone says, "I love God," yet hates his brother, he is a liar. For anyone who does not love his brother, whom he has seen, cannot love God, whom he has not seen. And he has given us this command: Whoever loves God must also love his brother.

1 John 4:20–21

As we have opportunity, let us do good to all people, especially to those who belong to the family of believers.

Galatians 6:10

How great is the love the Father has lavished on us, that we should be called children of God! And that is what we are!

1 John 3:1

God's Words of Life on
FAMILY RELATIONSHIPS

Sons are a heritage from the LORD,
  children a reward from him.
Like arrows in the hands of a warrior
  are sons born in one's youth.
Blessed is the man whose quiver is full of them.

Psalm 127:3–5

Jesus said, "Whatever you did for one of the least of these brothers of mine, you did for me."

Matthew 25:40

Do not forget the things your eyes have seen or let them slip from your heart as long as you live. Teach them to your children and to their children after them.

Deuteronomy 4:9

Jesus said, "Let the little children come to me, and do not hinder them, for the kingdom of God belongs to such as these."

Mark 10:14

All your sons will be taught by the LORD, and great will be your children's peace.

Isaiah 54:13

Young men ... be submissive to those who are older. All of you, clothe yourselves with humility toward one another.

1 Peter 5:5

God's Words of Life on
FAMILY RELATIONSHIPS

I have no greater joy than to hear that my children are walking in the truth.

3 John 1:4

We have all had human fathers who disciplined us and we respected them for it. How much more should we submit to the Father of our spirits and live! Our fathers disciplined us for a little while as they thought best; but God disciplines us for our good, that we may share in his holiness.

Hebrews 12:9–10

We dealt with each of you as a father deals with his own children, encouraging, comforting and urging you to live lives worthy of God, who calls you into his kingdom and glory.

1 Thessalonians 2:11–12

When we were children, we were in slavery under the basic principles of the world. But when the time had fully come, God sent his Son, born of a woman, born under law, to redeem those under law, that we might receive the full rights of sons. Because you are sons, God sent the Spirit of his Son into our hearts, the Spirit who calls out, *"Abba,* Father." So you are no longer a slave, but a son; and since you are a son, God has made you also an heir.

Galatians 4:3–7

Devotional Thought on
FAMILY RELATIONSHIPS

THE GIFT OF FAMILY

Your family is a gift from God to you. He wants you to know that, besides himself, these are the best people for you to receive love from and give love to. And he wants you to know how to live with your family in a way that is loving, kind and best for everybody.

God's design is for your family to teach you about God. If your parents are Christians, ask them to tell you about their faith. If your parents aren't Christians, God will work in other ways to teach you.

God wants you to respect and obey your parents. This is one of the BIGGIES in the Bible (found in the Ten Commandments). To honor and respect your parents means to listen to them, to take them seriously and treat them as people you really care about.

Love is the key to having a great family. Don't wait for others to love you. Loving your family members is a good place for love to begin.

God's Words of Life on
FEAR

The LORD is my light and my salvation—
   whom shall I fear?
The LORD is the stronghold of my life—
   of whom shall I be afraid?

Psalm 27:1

In God I trust; I will not be afraid.
   What can man do to me?

Psalm 56:11

For he will command his angels concerning you
   to guard you in all your ways;
they will lift you up in their hands,
   so that you will not strike your foot against
      a stone.
You will tread upon the lion and the cobra;
   you will trample the great lion and the
      serpent.
"Because he loves me," says the LORD,
   "I will rescue him; I will protect him, for he
      acknowledges my name."

Psalm 91:11–14

You did not receive a spirit that makes you a
slave again to fear, but you received the Spirit
of sonship.

Romans 8:15

God did not give us a spirit of timidity, but a
spirit of power of love and of self-discipline.

2 Timothy 1:7

God's Words of Life on
FEAR

Do not fear, for I am with you; do not be dismayed, for I am your God. I will strengthen you and help you; I will uphold you with my righteous right hand.

Isaiah 41:10

Do not be afraid, little flock, for your Father has been pleased to give you the kingdom.

Luke 12:32

We say with confidence, "The Lord is my helper; I will not be afraid."

Hebrews 13:6

When the servant of the man of God got up and went out early the next morning, an army with horses and chariots had surrounded the city. "Oh, my lord, what shall we do," the servant asked. "Don't be afraid," the prophet answered. "Those who are with us are more than those who are with them." And Elisha prayed, "O Lord, open his eyes so he may see." Then the Lord opened the servant's eyes, and he looked and saw the hills full of horses and chariots of fire all around Elisha.

2 Kings 6:15–17

There is no fear in love. But perfect love drives out fear.

1 John 4:18

God's Words of Life on
FEAR

I will say of the LORD, "He is my refuge and my
 fortress,
 my God, in whom I trust." . . .
He will cover you with his feathers,
 and under his wings you will find refuge;
his faithfulness will be your shield and rampart.

Psalm 91:2, 4

When you lie down, you will not be afraid;
when you lie down, your sleep will be sweet.
Have no fear of sudden disaster or of the ruin
that overtakes the wicked, for the LORD will be
your confidence and will keep your foot from
being snared.

Proverbs 3:24–26

Even though I walk
 through the valley of the shadow of death,
I will fear no evil,
 for you are with me;
your rod and your staff,
 they comfort me.

Psalm 23:4

We know that in all things God works for the
good of those who love him, who have been
called according to his purpose. . . . What, then,
shall we say in response to this? If God is for
us, who can be against us?

Romans 8:28, 31

God's Words of Life on
FEAR

The LORD is with me; I will not be afraid.

Psalm 118:6

When I am afraid,
I will trust in you, LORD.

Psalm 56:3

The word of the LORD came to me, saying,

"Before I formed you in the womb I knew you,
before you were born I set you apart;
I appointed you as a prophet to the nations."

"Ah, Sovereign LORD," I said, "I do not
know how to speak; I am only a child."

But the LORD said to me, "Do not say, 'I am
only a child.' You must go to everyone I send
you to and say whatever I command you. Do
not be afraid of them, for I am with you and
will rescue you," declares the LORD.

Jeremiah 1:4–8

During the fourth watch of the night Jesus
went out to [the disciples], walking on the lake.
When the disciples saw him walking on the
lake, they were terrified. "It's a ghost," they
said, and cried out in fear. But Jesus immedi-
ately said to them: "Take courage! It is I. Don't
be afraid."

Matthew 14:25–27

God's Words of Life on
FEAR

For I am the LORD, your God,
    who takes hold of your right hand
and says to you, Do not fear;
    I will help you.

Isaiah 41:13

Surely God is my salvation;
    I will trust and not be afraid.
The LORD, the LORD, is my strength and my song;
    he has become my salvation.

Isaiah 12:2

You came near when I called you,
    and you said, "Do not fear."
O Lord, you took up my case;
    you redeemed my life.

Lamentations 3:57–58

Be strong and take heart,
    all you who hope in the LORD.

Psalm 31:24

Devotional Thought on
FEAR

NEVER FEAR!

The story of Moses proves that God is always there to help people through hard times. Moses' mother was scared that her baby would be killed, so she sent him down the river in a basket. She probably couldn't have done that if she didn't trust God to take care of her baby.

It's not easy to trust God when you're scared. And fear can make people do things that aren't very smart. When I was really little, my sisters played a trick on me. I was sitting on top of a table when my sisters turned off the lights and ran out of the room. I was so scared that I didn't know what to do. Finally, I decided to jump off the table. But instead of landing on the floor, I hit the door of our stereo cabinet, which was glass. I ended up needing stitches! I got hurt because I panicked. I would have been fine if I'd stayed calm and called for help.

I learned that getting all worked up when you're scared doesn't make things better. The best thing we can do is ask God for help and trust him to take care of us.

CHRIS

God's Words of Life on
FORGIVENESS

As far as the east is from the west,
   so far has he removed our transgressions
      from us.

Psalm 103:12

I will cleanse them from all the sin they have
committed against me and will forgive all their
sins of rebellion against me.

Jeremiah 33:8

Bear with each other and forgive whatever
grievances you may have against one another.
Forgive as the Lord forgave you.

Colossians 3:13

"Come now, let us reason together," says the
LORD. "Though your sins are like scarlet, they
shall be as white as snow; though they are red
as crimson, they shall be like wool."

Isaiah 1:18

God was reconciling the world to himself in
Christ, not counting men's sins against them.
And he has committed to us the message of
reconciliation.

2 Corinthians 5:19

"I, even I, am he who blots out your transgressions, for my own sake, and remembers your
sins no more," says the Lord.

Isaiah 43:25

God's Words of Life on
FORGIVENESS

Blessed is he
    whose transgressions are forgiven,
    whose sins are covered.
Blessed is the man
    whose sin the LORD does not count against
        him
    and in whose spirit is no deceit.

Psalm 32:1–2

Peter came to Jesus and asked, "Lord, how many times shall I forgive my brother when he sins against me? Up to seven times?" Jesus answered, "I tell you, not seven times, but seventy-seven times."

Matthew 18:21–22

In Jesus we have redemption through his blood, the forgiveness of sins, in accordance with the riches of God's grace that he lavished on us with all wisdom and understanding.

Ephesians 1:7–8

You are forgiving and good, O Lord,
    abounding in love to all who call to you.

Psalm 86:5

The Lord our God is merciful and forgiving, even though we have rebelled against him.

Daniel 9:9

God's Words of Life on
FORGIVENESS

Who is a God like you, who pardons sin ...
You do not stay angry forever but delight to
show mercy.

Micah 7:18

If we walk in the light, as he is in the light, we
have fellowship with one another, and the blood
of Jesus, his Son, purifies us from all sin. If we
claim to be without sin, we deceive ourselves
and the truth is not in us. If we confess our sins,
he is faithful and just and will forgive us our
sins and purify us from all unrighteousness.

1 John 1:7-9

Remember not the sins of my youth
　　and my rebellious ways; according to your
　　　　love remember me,
for you are good, O LORD.

Psalm 25:7

You, O Lord, are a compassionate and gracious
　　God,
　　slow to anger, abounding in love and faith-
　　　　fulness.

Psalm 86:15

Praise the LORD,
　　O my soul, and forget not all his benefits—
who forgives all your sins
　　and heals all your diseases.

Psalm 103:2-3

God's Words of Life on
FORGIVENESS

Forgive all our sins and receive us graciously, that we may offer the fruit of our lips.

Hosea 14:2

Forgive us our debts, as we also have forgiven our debtors. And lead us not into temptation, but deliver us from the evil one.

Matthew 6:12–13

He who conceals his sins does not prosper, but whoever confesses and renounces them finds mercy.

Proverbs 28:13

Jesus said, "If your brother sins, rebuke him, and if he repents, forgive him. If he sins against you seven times in a day, and seven times comes back to you and says, 'I repent,' forgive him."

Luke 17:3

For the sake of your name, O LORD,
     forgive my iniquity, though it is great.

Psalm 25:11

Jesus said, "If you forgive men when they sin against you, your heavenly Father will also forgive you. But if you do not forgive men their sins, your Father will not forgive your sins."

Matthew 6:14–15

God's Words of Life on
FORGIVENESS

Be kind and compassionate to one another,
forgiving each other, just as in Christ God forgave you.

Ephesians 4:32

Forgive, and you will be forgiven.

Luke 6:37

I will sprinkle clean water on you, and you will
be clean; I will cleanse you from all your
impurities and from all your idols. I will give
you a new heart and put a new spirit in you; I
will remove from you your heart of stone and
give you a heart of flesh.

Ezekiel 36:25–26

Wash away all my iniquity
    and cleanse me from my sin.

Psalm 51:2

When we were overwhelmed by sins,
    you forgave our transgressions.

Psalm 65:3

Your sins have been forgiven on account of
Jesus' name.

1 John 2:12

Devotional Thought on
FORGIVENESS

REPEATED FORGIVENESS

Have you ever been wandering around the mall and bumped into someone you treated poorly? You know, that former friend you ditched, only because your other friends thought she was a real loser? Now you can't avoid running straight into her (you think about ducking into the next store until you realize it's a maternity shop). Talk about uncomfortable. What can you say? What can you do?

Remember the story of Jacob and Esau—the stolen birthright brothers? Did you know that Jacob later bumped into his brother Esau in the middle of nowhere? Jacob thought he was going to get the tar beat out of him, but instead Esau embraced him—it was forgive and forget. In that moment Jacob experienced the wonder of forgiveness.

We're supposed to forgive other people over and over and over again. Has anyone ever forgiven you for something you did? Didn't it feel great?

Imagine how it would feel if that former friend in the mall looked at you with forgiveness in her eyes instead of revenge. It would feel good, wouldn't it? Now it's your turn.

God's Words of Life on
FRIENDS

A friend loves at all times, and a brother is born for adversity.

Proverbs 17:17

I no longer call you servants, because a servant does not know his master's business. Instead, I have called you friends, for everything that I learned from my Father I have made known to you.

John 15:15

He who covers over an offense promotes love, but whoever repeats the matter separates close friends.

Proverbs 17:9

There is a friend who sticks closer than a brother.

Proverbs 18:24

Wounds from a friend can be trusted, but an enemy multiplies kisses.

Proverbs 27:6

Jesus said, "Greater love has no one than this, that he lay down his life for his friends. You are my friends if you do what I command."

John 15:13–14

Perfume and incense bring joy to the heart, and the pleasantness of one's friend springs from his earnest counsel.

Proverbs 27:9

God's Words of Life on
FRIENDS

Two are better than one, because they have a good return for their work: If one falls down, his friend can help him up. But pity the man who falls and has no one to help him up!

Ecclesiastes 4:9–10

Do not think of yourself more highly than you ought, but rather think of yourself with sober judgment, in accordance with the measure of faith God has given you. Just as each of us has one body with many members, and these members do not all have the same function, so in Christ we who are many form one body, and each member belongs to all the others.

Romans 12:3–5

Though one may be overpowered, two can defend themselves. A cord of three strands is not quickly broken.

Ecclesiastes 4:12

Be completely humble and gentle; be patient, bearing with one another in love. Make every effort to keep the unity of the Spirit through the bond of peace.

Ephesians 4:2–3

Carry each other's burdens, and in this way you will fulfill the law of Christ.

Galatians 6:2

God's Words of Life on
FRIENDS

Love one another deeply, from the heart.

1 Peter 1:22

Agree with one another so that there may be no divisions among you and that you may be perfectly united in mind and thought.

1 Corinthians 1:10

May the God who gives endurance and encouragement give you a spirit of unity among yourselves as you follow Christ Jesus, so that with one heart and mouth you may glorify the God and Father of our Lord Jesus Christ. Accept one another, then, just as Christ accepted you, in order to bring praise to God.

Romans 15:5–7

Keep on loving each other.

Hebrews 13:1

Devotional Thought on
FRIENDS

FOREVER FRIENDS

A real friend is a friend forever, not just for a summer or until you get out of the class you have together. And a real friend is loyal and faithful.

In 1 Samuel we read that Jonathan's dad, Saul, hated David. Saul was jealous of David's looks, popularity and the way people treated him. So Jonathan was torn between his dad and his best friend. When push came to shove, Jonathan proved to be a really committed friend. That's really the kind of relationship David and Jonathan had—they would do anything for each other.

Life is tough, and there are so many "enemies" around (enemies like loneliness, fear, distrust, to name a few) that we all need a good friend. The Bible gives us a great picture of what a friend is—not just someone to help *you* out, but someone you can help. Sometimes your friends need you a lot more than you need them. And that's OK, because we all go through times when we need somebody to come through for us and don't have much to give back.

Let David and Jonathan teach you what it means to be a great friend.

God's Words of Life on
GIVING

Freely you have received, freely give.

Matthew 10:8

They had given freely and wholeheartedly to the LORD.

1 Chronicles 29:9

We must help the weak, remembering the words the Lord Jesus himself said: "It is more blessed to give than to receive."

Acts 20:35

Do not forget to do good and to share with others, for with such sacrifices God is pleased.

Hebrews 13:16

He who supplies seed to the sower and bread for food will also supply and increase your store of seed and will enlarge the harvest of your righteousness. You will be made rich in every way so that you can be generous on every occasion, and through us your generosity will result in thanksgiving to God. This service that you perform is not only supplying the needs of God's people but is also overflowing in many expressions of thanks to God. Because of the service by which you have proved yourselves, men will praise God for the obedience that accompanies your confession of the gospel of Christ, and for your generosity in sharing with them and with everyone else.

2 Corinthians 9:10–13

God's Words of Life on
GIVING

Be openhanded and freely lend [your poor brother] whatever he needs. ... Give generously to him and do so without a grudging heart; then because of this the LORD your God will bless you in all your work and in everything you put your hand to.

Deuteronomy 15:8, 10

Remember this: Whoever sows sparingly will also reap sparingly, and whoever sows generously will also reap generously. Each man should give what he has decided in his heart to give, not reluctantly or under compulsion, for God loves a cheerful giver. And God is able to make all grace abound to you, so that in all things at all times, having all that you need, you will abound in every good work.

2 Corinthians 9:6–8

God is not unjust; he will not forget your work and the love you have shown him as you have helped his people and continue to help them.

Hebrews 6:10

As we have opportunity, let us do good to all people, especially to those who belong to the family of believers.

Galatians 6:10

God's Words of Life on
GIVING

Jesus said, "Give, and it will be given to you. A good measure, pressed down, shaken together and running over, will be poured into your lap. For with the measure you use, it will be measured to you."

Luke 6:38

At the present time your plenty will supply what they need, so that in turn their plenty will supply what you need. Then there will be equality, as it is written: "He who gathered much did not have too much, and he who gathered little did not have too little."

2 Corinthians 8:14–15

Give to everyone who asks you, and if anyone takes what belongs to you, do not demand it back.

Luke 6:30

Jesus said, "If anyone gives even a cup of cold water to one of these little ones because he is my disciple, I tell you the truth, he will certainly not lose his reward."

Matthew 10:42

A generous man will himself be blessed, for he shares his food with the poor.

Proverbs 22:9

God's Words of Life on
GIVING

He who refreshes others will himself be refreshed.

Proverbs 11:25

If you spend yourselves in behalf of the hungry and satisfy the needs of the oppressed, then your light will rise in the darkness, and your night will become like the noonday. The Lord will guide you always; he will satisfy your needs in a sun-scorched land and will strengthen your frame. You will be like a well-watered garden, like a spring whose waters never fail.

Isaiah 58:10–11

Jesus said, "The King will say, 'I was thirsty and you gave me something to drink, I was a stranger and you invited me in, I needed clothes and you clothed me, I was sick and you looked after me, I was in prison and you came to visit me.'
Then the righteous will answer him, 'Lord, when did we see you hungry and feed you, or thirsty and give you something to drink? When did we see you a stranger and invite you in, or needing clothes and clothe you? When did we see you sick or in prison and go to visit you?'
The King will reply, 'I tell you the truth, whatever you did for one of the least of these brothers of mine, you did for me.'"

Matthew 25:35–40

God's Words of Life on
GIVING

Love your enemies, do good to them, and lend to them without expecting to get anything back. Then your reward will be great, and you will be sons of the Most High.

Luke 6:35

He who is kind to the poor lends to the LORD, and he will reward him for what he has done.

Proverbs 19:17

The blessing of the LORD brings wealth, and he adds no trouble to it.

Proverbs 10:22

Honor the LORD with your wealth, with the firstfruits of all your crops; then your barns will be filled to overflowing, and your vats will brim over with new wine.

Proverbs 3:9–10

One man gives freely, yet gains even more; another withholds unduly, but comes to poverty.

Proverbs 11:24

Peter said, "Silver or gold I do not have, but what I have I give you."

Acts 3:6

Devotional Thought on
GIVING

SHARING WITH OTHERS

When I'm eating lunch in the cafeteria, sometimes I see that someone else has forgotten their lunch or forgotten to bring money to buy one. I should probably share some of my food with them. Often I think, *If I share my lunch, then I'll be hungry later.* But that's really no excuse. If I *don't* share my lunch, then the other kid will definitely be hungry later. I need to think about other people, because God cares for them as much as he cares for me. And if God cares, I should care too.

There are actually lots of good things that can come from sharing with other people. Once I start caring for people who have less than I do, I bet I'll want to do it more. And maybe other people will watch what I'm doing, and they'll want to do their part too. Next time I see someone who needs a hand, I'll try to help out.

KENT

God's Words of Life on
GOD'S WILL

In all your ways acknowledge him, and he will make your paths straight.

Proverbs 3:6

Commit to the LORD whatever you do, and your plans will succeed.

Proverbs 16:3

What does the LORD require of you? To act justly and to love mercy and to walk humbly with your God.

Micah 6:8

It is God who works in you to will and to act according to his good purpose.

Philippians 2:13

I will instruct you and teach you in the way
         you should go;
    I will counsel you and watch over you.

Psalm 32:8

Stand at the crossroads and look; ask for the ancient paths, ask where the good way is, and walk in it.

Jeremiah 6:16

All the days ordained for me were written in your book before one of them came to be.

Psalm 139:16

God's Words of Life on
GOD'S WILL

Come, let us go up to the mountain of the LORD, to the house of the God of Jacob. He will teach us his ways, so that we may walk in his paths.

Isaiah 2:3

"For I know the plans I have for you," declares the LORD, "plans to prosper you and not to harm you, plans to give you hope and a future."

Jeremiah 29:11

If you call out for insight and cry aloud for understanding, and if you look for it as for silver and search for it as for hidden treasure, then you will understand the fear of the LORD and find the knowledge of God.

Proverbs 2:3–5

Do not conform any longer to the pattern of this world, but be transformed by the renewing of your mind. Then you will be able to test and approve what God's will is—his good, pleasing and perfect will.

Romans 12:2

It is God's will that you should be sanctified.

1 Thessalonians 4:3

Those who suffer according to God's will should commit themselves to their faithful Creator and continue to do good.

1 Peter 4:19

God's Words of Life on
GOD'S WILL

I desire to do your will, O my God;
　　your law is within my heart.

Psalm 40:8

Teach me to do your will,
　　for you are my God;
may your good Spirit
　　lead me on level ground.

Psalm 143:10

Jesus said, "Whoever does the will of my
Father in heaven is my brother and sister and
mother."

Matthew 12:50

"For my thoughts are not your thoughts, neither are your ways my ways," declares the
LORD. "As the heavens are higher than the
earth, so are my ways higher than your ways
and my thoughts than your thoughts."

Isaiah 55:8–9

The LORD will fulfill his purpose for me;
　　your love, O LORD, endures forever—
　　do not abandon the works of your hands.

Psalm 138:8

God who searches our hearts knows the mind
of the Spirit, because the Spirit intercedes for
the saints in accordance with God's will.

Romans 8:27

God's Words of Life on
GOD'S WILL

First seek the counsel of the LORD.

1 Kings 22:5

May my cry come before you, O LORD;
> give me understanding according to your
> word.

Psalm 119:169

Since the day we heard about you, we have not
stopped praying for you and asking God to fill
you with the knowledge of his will through all
spiritual wisdom and understanding.

Colossians 1:9

Jesus said, "If anyone chooses to do God's will,
he will find out whether my teaching comes
from God or whether I speak on my own."

John 7:17

It is God's will that by doing good you should
silence the ignorant talk of foolish men.

1 Peter 2:15

It is better, if it is God's will, to suffer for doing
good than for doing evil.

1 Peter 3:17

You guide me with your counsel.

Psalm 73:24

God's Words of Life on
GOD'S WILL

And we know that in all things God works for the good of those who love him, who have been called according to his purpose.

Romans 8:28

The world and its desires pass away, but the man who does the will of God lives forever.

1 John 2:17

The plans of the LORD stand firm forever, the purposes of his heart through all generations.

Psalm 33:11

In his heart a man plans his course, but the LORD determines his steps.

Proverbs 16:9

God's Wonderful Map

God, your heavenly Father, has an incredible plan for your life, and he's given you a wonderful map—the Bible, the guide for your path. But you have to read it, learn it and apply it to your life.

It's God's responsibility to make sure we "get" his plan; it's our responsibility to communicate with him often. But communicating with God means more than just talking to him. We've got to listen too.

God uses other ways to show us his will. He works through our thoughts, our interests, our spiritual leaders and our gifts. God has given you specific gifts and abilities to use for his glory. So use 'em!

It's important to remember that "God's will" doesn't simply mean what your career will be, whom you'll marry and where you'll live. Those things are only parts of his will. His plan for you includes the things going on in your life right now, at this very moment. So instead of asking God what he wants you to do five years from now, ask him, "Lord, help me to be all you want me to be. What is your will for me today?"

Susie Shellenberger

God's Words of Life on
GOSSIP

May the words of my mouth and the meditation of my heart be pleasing in your sight, O LORD, my Rock and my Redeemer.

Psalm 19:14

The words of a gossip are like choice morsels; they go down to a man's inmost parts.

Proverbs 18:8

Without wood a fire goes out; without gossip a quarrel dies down.

Proverbs 26:20

Reckless words pierce like a sword, but the tongue of the wise brings healing.

Proverbs 12:18

A gossip betrays a confidence; so avoid a man who talks too much.

Proverbs 20:19

Do not let any unwholesome talk come out of your mouths, but only what is helpful for building others up.

Ephesians 4:29

Set a guard over my mouth, O LORD;
    keep watch over the door of my lips.
Let not my heart be drawn to what is evil,
    to take part in wicked deeds.

Psalm 141:3–4

God's Words of Life on
GOSSIP

A gossip separates close friends.

Proverbs 16:28

In everything, do to others what you would have them do to you.

Matthew 7:12

A gossip betrays a confidence, but a trustworthy man keeps a secret.

Proverbs 11:13

Whoever would love life and see good days must keep his tongue from evil and his lips from deceitful speech.

1 Peter 3:10

With the tongue we praise our Lord and Father, and with it we curse men, who have been made in God's likeness. Out of the same mouth come praise and cursing. ... This should not be. Can both fresh water and salt water flow from the same spring? ... Can a fig tree bear olives, or a grapevine bear figs? Neither can a salt spring produce fresh water.

James 3:9–12

As a north wind brings rain,
    so a sly tongue brings angry looks.

Proverbs 25:23

God's Words of Life on
GOSSIP

He who guards his mouth and his tongue
keeps himself from calamity.

Proverbs 21:23

The tongue that brings healing is a tree of life,
but a deceitful tongue crushes the spirit.

Proverbs 15:4

When words are many, sin is not absent,
but he who holds his tongue is wise.

Proverbs 10:19

If anyone speaks, he should do it as one speaking the very words of God.

1 Peter 4:11

Live in harmony with one another; be sympathetic, love as brothers, be compassionate and
humble. Do not repay evil with evil or insult
with insult, but with blessing, because to this
you were called so that you may inherit a
blessing.

1 Peter 3:8–9

Devotional Thought on
GOSSIP

REGRETTABLE WORDS

I've said some things in my life that I've regretted. One of the biggest things I regret saying involves a girl I hardly knew. When I was with a bunch of my friends at a slumber party, I started gossiping about this girl—talking about her behind her back and saying things about her that just weren't true. Eventually she found out, and I lost the chance to ever be her friend. I tried to make things right, but she never said another word to me.

It was low of me to try to impress my friends by gossiping about an innocent person. Proverbs 3:29 says that I should not do any harm to the people around me. When I gossiped about this girl, I hurt her, and I hurt God too. God created each person in a special way. When we make fun of someone, it's like we're telling God, "That girl or guy isn't good enough for me." And how can we do that when that person is good enough for God?

MEGAN

God's Words of Life on
JOY

My servants will sing out of the joy of their hearts.

Isaiah 65:14

Light is shed upon the righteous
   and joy on the upright in heart.

Psalm 97:11

He will yet fill your mouth with laughter and your lips with shouts of joy.

Job 8:21

God's favor lasts a lifetime;
   weeping may remain for a night,
but rejoicing comes in the morning.

Psalm 30:5

Rejoice in the LORD and be glad, you righteous;
   sing, all you who are upright in heart!

Psalm 32:11

Let the righteous rejoice in the LORD
   and take refuge in him;
let all the upright in heart praise him!

Psalm 64:10

Jesus said, "As the Father has loved me, so have I loved you. Now remain in my love. ... I have told you this so that my joy may be in you and that your joy may be complete."

John 15:9, 11

God's Words of Life on
JOY

May the righteous be glad
    and rejoice before God;
may they be happy and joyful.

Psalm 68:3

May all who seek you
    rejoice and be glad in you;
may those who love your salvation always say,
    "Let God be exalted!"

Psalm 70:4

The ransomed of the LORD will return. They
will enter Zion with singing; everlasting joy
will crown their heads. Gladness and joy will
overtake them, and sorrow and sighing will
flee away.

Isaiah 51:11

Let all who take refuge in you be glad;
    let them ever sing for joy.
Spread your protection over them,
    that those who love your name may rejoice
        in you.

Psalm 5:11

Shout for joy to the LORD,
    all the earth.
Worship the LORD with gladness;
    come before him with joyful songs.

Psalm 100:1–2

God's Words of Life on
Joy

I rejoice in following your statutes
   as one rejoices in great riches.

Psalm 119:14

Those who sow in tears
   will reap with songs of joy.

Psalm 126:5

The prospect of the righteous is joy.

Proverbs 10:28

You will go out in joy and be led forth in
peace; the mountains and hills will burst into
song before you, and all the trees of the field
will clap their hands.

Isaiah 55:12

Rejoice in the Lord your God, for he has given
you the autumn rains in righteousness. He
sends you abundant showers, both autumn and
spring rains, as before.

Joel 2:23

Jesus said, "Until now you have not asked for
anything in my name. Ask and you will
receive, and your joy will be complete."

John 16:24

You have made known to me the paths of life;
you will fill me with joy in your presence.

Acts 2:28

God's Words of Life on
JOY

Rejoice in the Lord always. I will say it again: Rejoice!

Philippians 4:4

Be joyful always.

1 Thessalonians 5:16

May the God of hope fill you with all joy and peace as you trust in him, so that you may overflow with hope by the power of the Holy Spirit.

Romans 15:13

The joy of the LORD is your strength.

Nehemiah 8:10

Let the heavens rejoice, let the earth be glad; let them say among the nations, "The LORD reigns!" Let the sea resound, and all that is in it; let the fields be jubilant, and everything in them! Then the trees of the forest will sing, they will sing for joy before the LORD.

1 Chronicles 16:31–33

A cheerful look brings joy to the heart, and good news gives health to the bones.

Proverbs 15:30

Be happy ... while you are young, and let your heart give you joy in the days of your youth.

Ecclesiastes 11:9

God's Words of Life on
JOY

Maidens will dance and be glad, young men
and old as well. I will turn their mourning into
gladness; I will give them comfort and joy
instead of sorrow.

Jeremiah 31:13

To him who is able to keep you from falling
and to present you before his glorious presence
without fault and with great joy—to the only
God our Savior be glory, majesty, power and
authority, through Jesus Christ our Lord, before
all ages, now and forevermore! Amen.

Jude 24–25

The LORD your God will bless you in ... all the
work of your hands, and your joy will be complete.

Deuteronomy 16:15

Though you have not seen Christ, you love
him; and even though you do not see him now,
you believe in him and are filled with an inexpressible and glorious joy, for you are receiving the goal of your faith, the salvation of your
souls.

1 Peter 1:8–9

Devotional Thought on
Joy

PARTY ON TO JOY!

I've been to parties that made me feel really horrible and low because everybody there was just putting on a show, getting all worried about how they looked and who paid attention to them. I've also been to parties that made me feel really happy because people were just being themselves and having a ton of fun. Most of the fun parties were youth group parties—but when I tell my other friends how much fun I had, they don't believe me!

Some of my friends think of God as a head honcho who sits on a big throne and orders people to "be good." I used to think of God that way too. But youth group activities, and verses like Nehemiah 8:10, show me that God wants us to have fun too. He created a beautiful world for us, and I guess you could say he created fun. It's all part of the great life he wants us to have.

When I find my joy in God, my friends will see it. And maybe they'll want that joy too.

CARISSA

God's Words of Life on
LONELINESS

The LORD your God goes with you; he will never leave you nor forsake you.

Deuteronomy 31:6

God sets the lonely in families.

Psalm 68:6

I am always with you;
   you hold me by my right hand.

Psalm 73:23

Jesus said, "Surely I am with you always, to the very end of the age."

Matthew 28:20

Jesus said, "I will not leave you as orphans; I will come to you."

John 14:18

In Christ we who are many form one body, and each member belongs to all the others.

Romans 12:5

You are with me; your rod and your staff, they comfort me.

Psalm 23:4

Paul said, "At my first defense, no one came to my support, but everyone deserted me. May it not be held against them. But the Lord stood at my side and gave me strength."

2 Timothy 4:16–17

God's Words of Life on
LONELINESS

God said, "I am with you and will watch over you wherever you go ... I will not leave you until I have done what I have promised you."

Genesis 28:15

Those who know your name will trust in you, for you, LORD, have never forsaken those who seek you.

Psalm 9:10

Come near to God and he will come near to you.

James 4:8

Jesus said, "Do not let your hearts be troubled. Trust in God; trust also in me."

John 14:1

The LORD heals the brokenhearted and binds up their wounds.

Psalm 147:3

Though my father and mother forsake me, the LORD will receive me.

Psalm 27:10

"Though the mountains be shaken and the hills be removed, yet my unfailing love for you will not be shaken nor my covenant of peace be removed," says the LORD, who has compassion on you.

Isaiah 54:10

God's Words of Life on
LONELINESS

May the Lord of peace himself give you peace at all times and in every way. The Lord be with all of you.

2 Thessalonians 3:16

For I am convinced that neither death nor life, neither angels nor demons, neither the present nor the future, nor any powers, neither height nor depth, nor anything else in all creation, will be able to separate us from the love of God that is in Christ Jesus our Lord.

Romans 8:38–39

Praise be to God,
who has not rejected my prayer
or withheld his love from me!

Psalm 66:20

I call to God,
and the LORD saves me.

Psalm 55:16

So do not fear, for I am with you;
do not be dismayed, for I am your God.
I will strengthen you and help you;
I will uphold you with my righteous right
hand.

Isaiah 41:10

Devotional Thought on
LONELINESS

A CURE FOR LONELINESS

It sometimes seems like everybody else has a best friend, a cool friend's party to go to or more e-mail messages than you do. If you've ever felt lonely, you're not alone. You're actually surrounded by tons of others who feel just like you do. Next time you feel lonely, try to remember some of what the Bible says:

If you want to have good friends, you need to be a good friend. We're always waiting for other people to take the first step and call us or be nice to us. Guess what? They're waiting for us to make the first move. So why not make the first phone call (Matthew 7:12)?

There's always someone else without a friend. Remember that there are tons of other kids who are probably feeling lonely just like you. Hook up with one of them (Ecclesiastes 4:9–12).

You always have one important friend. JESUS is a friend who's with you all the time (Proverbs 18:24). He's with you as you read this. And he'll be with you when you put this down. The God of the universe is just waiting to spend time with you. Have a blast hanging out with him today!

God's Words of Life on
LOVING OTHERS

Since God so loved us, we also ought to love one another. No one has ever seen God; but if we love one another, God lives in us and his love is made complete in us.

1 John 4:11–12

This is how we know what love is: Jesus Christ laid down his life for us. And we ought to lay down our lives for our brothers . . . Let us not love with words or tongue but with actions and in truth.

1 John 3:16,18

Above all, love each other deeply, because love covers over a multitude of sins.

1 Peter 4:8

Let us love one another, for love comes from God. Everyone who loves has been born of God and knows God. Whoever does not love does not know God, because God is love.

1 John 4:7–8

Jesus said, "Greater love has no one than this, that he lay down his life for his friends."

John 15:13

Be devoted to one another in brotherly love.

Romans 12:10

God's Words of Life on
LOVING OTHERS

Love is patient, love is kind. It does not envy, it does not boast, it is not proud. It is not rude, it is not self-seeking, it is not easily angered, it keeps no record of wrongs. Love does not delight in evil but rejoices with the truth. It always protects, always trusts, always hopes, always perseveres.

1 Corinthians 13:4–7

How good and pleasant it is
    when brothers live together in unity!

Psalm 133:1

Live a life of love, just as Christ loved us and gave himself up for us as a fragrant offering and sacrifice to God.

Ephesians 5:2

May the Lord make your love increase and overflow for each other and for everyone else.

1 Thessalonians 3:12

About brotherly love we do not need to write to you, for you yourselves have been taught by God to love each other.

1 Thessalonians 4:9

Keep on loving each other.

Hebrews 13:1

God's Words of Life on
LOVING OTHERS

If you really keep the royal law found in Scripture, "Love your neighbor as yourself," you are doing right.

James 2:8

Jesus said, "As I have loved you, so you must love one another. By this all men will know that you are my disciples, if you love one another."

John 13:34–35

Love one another deeply, from the heart.

1 Peter 1:22

Live in harmony with one another; be sympathetic, love as brothers, be compassionate and humble.

1 Peter 3:8

The only thing that counts is faith expressing itself through love.

Galatians 5:6

Devotional Thought on
LOVING OTHERS

THE RIGHT STUFF

Attitude is more important than actions. You can do all the right things but still have a bad attitude, and the right things won't mean anything. The apostle Paul even said in 1 Corinthians 13 that you can die for God, but if you don't have love, it's worthless.

Jesus makes it very clear that the main way people can recognize his followers is by their really huge Bibles. No, wait, that's not it—it's by, um, their church attendance. Oh—that's not it either. The truth is, Jesus says people can recognize his followers by their love for each other.

What Jesus wants are disciples who love one another, not necessarily disciples who live perfect lives. That's why the gospel is called "Good News." Jesus knows all about our behavior and our actions. But, just as much, he knows our hearts—he knows what we're thinking and why we do what we do.

So cheer up! Maybe your actions aren't always what you want them to be, but if you love Jesus and care deeply about him, he knows about it. Your love for him and others is what matters most.

God's Words of Life on
LYING

Do not lie to each other, since you have taken off your old self with its practices.

Colossians 3:9

Whoever of you loves life and desires to see many good days, keep your tongue from evil and your lips from speaking lies.

Psalm 34:12–13

Truthful lips endure forever,
    but a lying tongue lasts only a moment.
There is deceit in the hearts of those who plot evil,
    but joy for those who promote peace.
No harm befalls the righteous,
    but the wicked have their fill of trouble.
The LORD detests lying lips,
    but he delights in men who are truthful.

Proverbs 12:19–22

These are the things you are to do: Speak the truth to each other, and render true and sound judgment.

Zechariah 8:16

Each of you must put off falsehood and speak truthfully to his neighbor, for we are all members of one body.

Ephesians 4:25

God's Words of Life on
LYING

If anyone speaks, he should do it as one speaking the very words of God.

1 Peter 4:11

Words from a wise man's mouth are gracious,
but a fool is consumed by his own lips.

Ecclesiastes 10:12

Do not be quick with your mouth,
do not be hasty in your heart.

Ecclesiastes 5:2

Two things I ask of you, O LORD; ...
Keep falsehood and lies far from me;
give me neither poverty nor riches,
but give me only my daily bread.

Proverbs 30:7–8

Apply your heart to instruction
and your ears to words of knowledge.

Proverbs 23:12

Reckless words pierce like a sword,
but the tongue of the wise brings healing.

Proverbs 12:18

Do your best to present yourself to God as one approved ... who does not need to be ashamed and who correctly handles the word of truth.

2 Timothy 2:15

God's Words of Life on
LYING

Speaking the truth in love, we will in all things grow up into him who is the Head, that is, Christ.

Ephesians 4:15

Love does not delight in evil but rejoices with the truth.

1 Corinthians 13:6

An honest answer is like a kiss on the lips.

Proverbs 24:26

If your heart is wise, then my heart will be glad; my inmost being will rejoice when your lips speak what is right.

Proverbs 23:15–16

Kings take pleasure in honest lips; they value a man who speaks the truth.

Proverbs 16:13

Devotional Thought on
Lying

Easy Lies

I remember the first time I lied to my parents. I knew what "sin" meant before that, but it was the first time I really felt like I had sinned. It was horrible.

I hated feeling so guilty, and I told myself I'd never lie again. But then I told another lie. I felt bad, but not quite so bad as the first time. Before I knew it, I was lying all the time. It was like I couldn't stop.

Even though lying got easier and easier, the guilty feeling never totally went away. That's when I learned that guilt isn't always a bad thing. The bad feeling made me want to stop lying.

Finally, I asked God to forgive me and help me stop lying. When I apologized to my parents and told them the truth, the horrible feeling went away. I definitely learned a lesson about sin and how important it is to ask for forgiveness. I just wish I hadn't had to learn it the hard way.

Zach

God's Words of Life on
MONEY

The love of money is a root of all kinds of evil. Some people, eager for money, have wandered from the faith and pierced themselves with many griefs.

1 Timothy 6:10

Wisdom is a shelter as money is a shelter, but the advantage of knowledge is this: that wisdom preserves the life of its possessor.

Ecclesiastes 7:12

Command those who are rich in this present world not to be arrogant nor to put their hope in wealth, which is so uncertain, but to put their hope in God, who richly provides us with everything for our enjoyment. Command them to do good, to be rich in good deeds, and to be generous and willing to share. In this way they will lay up treasure for themselves as a firm foundation for the coming age, so that they may take hold of the life that is truly life.

1 Timothy 6:17–19

Keep your lives free from the love of money and be content with what you have.

Hebrews 13:5

Do not charge your brother interest, whether on money or food or anything else that may earn interest.

Deuteronomy 23:19

God's Words of Life on
MONEY

Jesus said, "Love your enemies, do good to them, and lend to them without expecting to get anything back. Then your reward will be great, and you will be sons of the Most High."

Luke 6:35

If one of your countrymen becomes poor and is unable to support himself among you, help him ... so he can continue to live among you. Do not take interest of any kind from him, but fear your God, so that your countryman may continue to live among you. You must not lend him money at interest or sell him food at a profit. I am the LORD your God.

Leviticus 25:35–38

Jesus said, "Do not store up for yourselves treasures on earth, where moth and rust destroy, and where thieves break in and steal. But store up for yourselves treasures in heaven, where moth and rust do not destroy, and where thieves do not break in and steal."

Matthew 6:19–20

Remember the LORD your God, for it is he who gives you the ability to produce wealth ...

Deuteronomy 8:18

Jesus said, "Watch out! Be on your guard against all kinds of greed; a man's life does not consist in the abundance of his possessions."

Luke 12:15

God's Words of Life on
MONEY

Jesus said, "No one can serve two masters. Either he will hate the one and love the other, or he will be devoted to the one and despise the other. You cannot serve both God and Money."

Matthew 6:24

Whoever trusts in his riches will fall, but the righteous will thrive like a green leaf.

Proverbs 11:28

Jesus sat down opposite the place where the offerings were put and watched the crowd putting their money into the temple treasury. Many rich people threw in large amounts. But a poor widow came and put in two very small copper coins, worth only a fraction of a penny. Calling his disciples to him, Jesus said, "I tell you the truth, this poor widow has put more into the treasury than all the others. They all gave out of their wealth; but she, out of her poverty, put in everything—all she had to live on."

Mark 12:41–44

"Bring the whole tithe into the storehouse, that there may be food in my house. Test me in this," says the LORD Almighty, "and see if I will not throw open the floodgates of heaven and pour out so much blessing that you will not have room enough for it."

Malachi 3:10

Devotional Thought on
MONEY

SPENDING IT MY WAY

I wanted to buy a bike. My parents told me to think about my decision and make sure that this was what I really wanted to do with my money. But I didn't want anybody to tell me what to do, so I just went out and bought a bike without really looking into what I wanted and how much I should pay. I made a bad decision because I was too stubborn to listen to my parents.

I'm not always so great about listening to God either. I think most of us try to "carry out plans" that aren't God's. And every time we do, we're opening the door for big problems to come on in. If people—including me—would just realize that God's incredible wisdom can help us make good decisions, we could save ourselves a lot of trouble.

JON

God's Words of Life on
PATIENCE

Be still before the LORD
and wait patiently for him.

Psalm 37:7

The end of a matter is better than its beginning, and patience is better than pride.

Ecclesiastes 7:8

It is good to wait quietly for the salvation of the LORD.

Lamentations 3:26

Wait for the LORD;
be strong and take heart
and wait for the LORD.

Psalm 27:14

LORD, walking in the way of your laws, we wait for you; your name and renown are the desire of our hearts.

Isaiah 26:8

As God's chosen people, holy and dearly loved, clothe yourselves with compassion, kindness, humility, gentleness and patience.

Colossians 3:12

Be joyful in hope, patient in affliction, faithful in prayer.

Romans 12:12

God's Words of Life on
PATIENCE

If we hope for what we do not yet have, we wait for it patiently.

Romans 8:25

I wait for the LORD, my soul waits,
and in his word I put my hope.
My soul waits for the Lord
more than watchmen wait for the morning.

Psalm 130:5-6

Be patient, then, brothers, until the Lord's coming. See how the farmer waits for the land to yield its valuable crop and how patient he is for the autumn and spring rains. You too, be patient and stand firm, because the Lord's coming is near.

James 5:7-8

Be completely humble and gentle; be patient, bearing with one another in love.

Ephesians 4:2

The fruit of the Spirit is love, joy, peace, patience, kindness, goodness, faithfulness, gentleness and self-control. Against such things there is no law.

Galatians 5:22-23

Pursue righteousness, godliness, faith, love, endurance and gentleness.

1 Timothy 6:11

God's Words of Life on
PATIENCE

The LORD longs to be gracious to you; he rises to show you compassion. For the LORD is a God of justice. Blessed are all who wait for him!

Isaiah 30:18

The Lord is not slow in keeping his promise, as some understand slowness. He is patient with you.

2 Peter 3:9

A man's wisdom gives him patience;
   it is to his glory to overlook an offense.

Proverbs 19:11

As an example of patience in the face of suffering, take the prophets who spoke in the name of the Lord. As you know, we consider blessed those who have persevered. You have heard of Job's perseverance and have seen what the Lord finally brought about. The Lord is full of compassion and mercy.

James 5:10–11

I know what it is to be in need, and I know what it is to have plenty. I have learned the secret of being content in any and every situation, whether well fed or hungry, whether living in plenty or in want. I can do everything through God who gives me strength.

Philippians 4:12–13

God's Words of Life on
PATIENCE

Imitate those who through faith and patience inherit what has been promised.

Hebrews 6:12

I was shown mercy so that in me, the worst of sinners, Christ Jesus might display his unlimited patience as an example for those who would believe on him and receive eternal life.

1 Timothy 1:16

There is a time for everything, and a season for every activity under heaven ...
God has made everything beautiful in its time.

Ecclesiastes 3:1, 11

Humble yourselves ... under God's mighty hand, that he may lift you up in due time.

1 Peter 5:6

Let us not become weary in doing good, for at the proper time we will reap a harvest if we do not give up.

Galatians 6:9

Do not forget this one thing, dear friends: With the Lord a day is like a thousand years, and a thousand years are like a day. ... Bear in mind that our Lord's patience means salvation.

2 Peter 3:8, 15

God's Words of Life on
PATIENCE

As for me, I watch in hope for the LORD, I wait for God my Savior; my God will hear me.

Micah 7:7

Since ancient times no one has heard, no ear has perceived, no eye has seen any God besides you, who acts on behalf of those who wait for him.

Isaiah 64:4

Encourage the timid, help the weak, be patient with everyone.

1 Thessalonians 5:14

Preach the Word; be prepared in season and out of season; correct, rebuke and encourage— with great patience and careful instruction.

2 Timothy 4:2

In the morning, O LORD, you hear my voice; in the morning I lay my requests before you and wait in expectation.

Psalm 5:3

Devotional Thought on
PATIENCE

WAITING FOR GOD

About 4 years ago, my family joined a new, larger church. I didn't know anyone at first, and I asked God to provide new friends for me. God did provide some great friends eventually, but I can't say he came through exactly the way I asked him to. It took me almost two years to start making solid friendships.

Part of faith is being "certain of what we do not see" (Hebrews 11:1). For the longest time, I didn't see God working. But now that I have many good, Christian friends, I can look back and see he was there, helping me all along.

Sometimes it's hard to trust God and have the patience to wait for him. When I feel like God isn't listening, that's when I need to take verses like this one seriously. If I have faith in God's plan for me, he will see my faith and work everything out in his time.

MIKE

God's Words of Life on
PEER PRESSURE

Blessed is the [one] who does not walk in the counsel of the wicked or stand in the way of sinners or sit in the seat of mockers.

Psalm 1:1

No longer be infants, tossed back and forth by the waves, and blown here and there by every wind of teaching and by the cunning and craftiness of men in their deceitful scheming.

Ephesians 4:14

See to it that no one takes you captive through hollow and deceptive philosophy, which depends on human tradition and the basic principles of this world rather than on Christ.

Colossians 2:8

Jesus said, "I have set you an example that you should do as I have done."

John 13:15

If your very own brother, ... or your closest friend secretly entices you, saying, "Let us go and worship other gods" ... do not yield to him or listen to him.

Deuteronomy 13:6, 8

In everything set them an example by doing what is good.

Titus 2:7

God's Words of Life on
PEER PRESSURE

If sinners entice you, do not give in to them.

Proverbs 1:10

Do not be misled: "Bad company corrupts good character."

1 Corinthians 15:33

Am I now trying to win the approval of men, or of God? Or am I trying to please men? If I were still trying to please men, I would not be a servant of Christ.

Galatians 1:10

Do not let your heart envy sinners, but always be zealous for the fear of the LORD. There is surely a future hope for you, and your hope will not be cut off. Listen ... and be wise, and keep your heart on the right path.

Proverbs 23:17–19

Don't let anyone look down on you because you are young, but set an example for the believers in speech, in life, in love, in faith and in purity.

1 Timothy 4:12

Whether you eat or drink or whatever you do, do it all for the glory of God. Do not cause anyone to stumble.

1 Corinthians 10:31–32

God's Words of Life on
PEER PRESSURE

Follow the way of love.

1 Corinthians 14:1

May the God who gives endurance and encouragement give you a spirit of unity among yourselves as you follow Christ Jesus, so that with one heart and mouth you may glorify the God and Father of our Lord Jesus Christ. Accept one another, then, just as Christ accepted you, in order to bring praise to God.

Romans 15:5–7

We speak as men approved by God to be entrusted with the gospel. We are not trying to please men but God, who tests our hearts.

1 Thessalonians 2:4

Dear children, do not let anyone lead you astray. He who does what is right is righteous, just as God is righteous.

1 John 3:7

A righteous man is cautious in friendship,
    but the way of the wicked leads them astray.

Proverbs 12:26

PEER PRESSURE

PLEASING PEOPLE OR GOD?

The other day, my friends and I were sitting at the lunch table, just talking and joking around. I said something kind of sarcastic about one of my friends because I thought the other people would think it was funny. But I ended up hurting my friend's feelings instead.

There are a lot of things we do to try to impress other people or make them like us. Some people start smoking because other people will think it's cool. Some people swear or gossip or make fun of other people to seem funny or smart. But those things don't please God. Every day we have to decide if we want to follow the crowd or obey God. We can't always do both.

In the long run, it's much better for us to obey God. He loves us and gives us eternal life. Obeying him is our way of saying, "Thanks!"

LISA

God's Words of Life on
PRAYER

"Before they call I will answer;" says the Lord,
" while they are still speaking I will hear."

Isaiah 65:24

Jesus said, "Whatever you ask for in prayer,
believe that you have received it, and it will be
yours."

Mark 11:24

Ask and it will be given to you; seek and you
will find; knock and the door will be opened to
you. For everyone who asks receives; he who
seeks finds; and to him who knocks, the door
will be opened.

Matthew 7:7–8

Jesus said, "I tell you that if two of you on
earth agree about anything you ask for, it will
be done for you by my Father in heaven. For
where two or three come together in my name,
there am I with them."

Matthew 18:19–20

When you pray, go into your room, close the
door and pray to your Father, who is unseen.
Then your Father, who sees what is done in
secret, will reward you.

Matthew 6:6

The Lord is near to all who call on him,
to all who call on him in truth.

Psalm 145:18

God's Words of Life on
PRAYER

"Call to me and I will answer you and tell you great and unsearchable things you do not know," says the LORD.

Jeremiah 33:3

He will call upon me, and I will answer him;
    I will be with him in trouble,
I will deliver him and honor him.

Psalm 91:15

The LORD is far from the wicked but he hears the prayer of the righteous.

Proverbs 15:29

Delight yourself in the LORD
    and he will give you the desires of your
        heart.

Psalm 37:4

Let us then approach the throne of grace with confidence, so that we may receive mercy and find grace to help us in our time of need.

Hebrews 4:16

Jesus said, "I tell you the truth, my Father will give you whatever you ask in my name. Until now you have not asked for anything in my name. Ask and you will receive, and your joy will be complete."

John 16:23–24

God's Words of Life on
PRAYER

Jesus said, "If you remain in me and my words remain in you, ask whatever you wish, and it will be given you."

John 15:7

I wait for you, O LORD;
    you will answer, O Lord my God.

Psalm 38:15

If we confess our sins, he is faithful and just and will forgive us our sins and purify us from all unrighteousness.

1 John 1:9

Very early in the morning, while it was still dark, Jesus got up, left the house and went off to a solitary place, where he prayed.

Mark 1:35

Is any one of you in trouble? He should pray. Is anyone happy? Let him sing songs of praise. Is any one of you sick? He should call the elders of the church to pray over him and anoint him with oil in the name of the Lord. And the prayer offered in faith will make the sick person well; the Lord will raise him up. If he has sinned, he will be forgiven. Therefore confess your sins to each other and pray for each other so that you may be healed.

James 5:13–16

God's Words of Life on
PRAYER

This is the confidence we have in approaching God: that if we ask anything according to his will, he hears us. And if we know that he hears us—whatever we ask—we know that we have what we asked of him.

1 John 5:14–15

The eyes of the Lord are on the righteous and his ears are attentive to their prayer.

1 Peter 3:12

Answer me when I call to you,
    O my righteous God.
Give me relief from my distress;
    be merciful to me and hear my prayer.

Psalm 4:1

By day the Lord directs his love,
    at night his song is with me—
    a prayer to the God of my life.

Psalm 42:8

Jesus said, "This, then, is how you should pray: 'Our Father in heaven, hallowed be your name, your kingdom come, your will be done on earth as it is in heaven. Give us today our daily bread. Forgive us our debts, as we also have forgiven our debtors. And lead us not into temptation, but deliver us from the evil one.'"

Matthew 6:9–13

God's Words of Life on
PRAYER

Be faithful in prayer.

Romans 12:12

If my people, who are called by my name, will humble themselves and pray and seek my face and turn from their wicked ways, then will I hear from heaven and will forgive their sin and will heal their land.

2 Chronicles 7:14

Do not be anxious about anything, but in everything, by prayer and petition, with thanksgiving, present your requests to God. And the peace of God, which transcends all understanding, will guard your hearts and your minds in Christ Jesus.

Philippians 4:6–7

Devote yourselves to prayer, being watchful and thankful.

Colossians 4:2

Be joyful always; pray continually; give thanks in all circumstances, for this is God's will for you in Christ Jesus.

1 Thessalonians 5:16–18

SOMEONE WHO REALLY LISTENS

A few months ago, I was praying for my friend Annie. She had a serious back problem called scoliosis, and she was scared she might have to have surgery. So in my prayers, I asked God to heal Annie's back.

Well, a few weeks later, Annie's back started to get better. We were at camp and people were praying for her. The pain she'd felt for months started to go away. It was a complete miracle! Now she doesn't have to have surgery, and she feels so much better.

That whole experience proved to me that God really does answer prayers. We're not talking to a brick wall when we pray—we're talking to Someone who really listens. That doesn't mean God will answer our prayers right away or give us everything we ask for. But even if Annie had needed surgery, I know God still would have answered our prayers by keeping her safe.

JOSH

God's Words of Life on
PRIDE

This is what the LORD says: "Let not the wise man boast of his wisdom or the strong man boast of his strength or the rich man boast of his riches, but let him who boasts boast about this: that he understands and knows me, that I am the LORD, who exercises kindness, justice and righteousness on earth, for in these I delight," declares the LORD.

Jeremiah 9:23–24

Pride goes before destruction, a haughty spirit before a fall. Better to be lowly in spirit and among the oppressed than to share plunder with the proud.

Proverbs 16:18–19

Pride only breeds quarrels, but wisdom is found in those who take advice.

Proverbs 13:10

My soul will boast in the LORD.

Psalm 34:2

When pride comes, then comes disgrace, but with humility comes wisdom.

Proverbs 11:2

Before his downfall a man's heart is proud, but humility comes before honor.

Proverbs 18:12

God's Words of Life on
PRIDE

Jesus said, "For everyone who exalts himself will be humbled, and he who humbles himself will be exalted."

Luke 18:14

Do not think of yourself more highly than you ought.

Romans 12:3

Each one should test his own actions. Then he can take pride in himself, without comparing himself to somebody else, for each one should carry his own load.

Galatians 6:4–5

The brother in humble circumstances ought to take pride in his high position. . . .
Blessed is the man who perseveres under trial, because when he has stood the test, he will receive the crown of life that God has promised to those who love him.

James 1:9, 12

You save the humble
  but bring low those whose eyes are haughty.

Psalm 18:27

God guides the humble in what is right
  and teaches them his way.

Psalm 25:9

God's Words of Life on
PRIDE

"This is the one I esteem: he who is humble and contrite in spirit, and trembles at my word," declares the LORD.

Isaiah 66:2

Humble yourselves . . . under God's mighty hand, that he may lift you up in due time.

1 Peter 5:6

Live in harmony with one another; be sympathetic, love as brothers, be compassionate and humble.

1 Peter 3:8

My heart is not proud, O LORD, my eyes are not haughty; I do not concern myself with great matters or things too wonderful for me.

Psalm 131:1

God mocks proud mockers but gives grace to the humble.

Proverbs 3:34

[Love] does not envy, it does not boast, it is not proud.

1 Corinthians 13:4

STUCK UP WITH PRIDE

I remember when we were playing another school in basketball for the second time in one season. The first time we played them, I had a great game and scored somewhere between fifteen and twenty points. But when it was time for the second game, I was full of pride and played cocky. I ended up with four or six points, and we lost by about twenty-five.

Absalom had a different problem: He was stuck up about his appearance, and especially his hair. He must have been growing it out for a long time if he had enough of it to get caught in a tree. He probably thought he looked handsome until he was hanging in midair. Then I bet he looked pretty stupid.

No matter what it is you're overly proud about, that attitude's going to hurt you eventually. Besides, pride is totally opposite from what God wants us to be like. He wants us to be humble and not draw attention or glory to ourselves. Instead, we should glorify him.

DERRICK

God's Words of Life on
PRIORITIES

Do not worry saying, 'What shall we eat?' or 'What shall we drink?' or 'What shall we wear?' ... Seek first his kingdom and his righteousness, and all these things will be given to you as well.

Matthew 6:31, 33

Since we are surrounded by such a great cloud of witnesses, let us throw off everything that hinders and the sin that so easily entangles, and let us run with perseverance the race marked out for us. Let us fix our eyes on Jesus, the author and perfecter of our faith, who for the joy set before him endured the cross, scorning its shame, and sat down at the right hand of the throne of God.

Hebrews 12:1–2

Be faithful ... and I will give you the crown of life.

Revelation 2:10

By faith Moses, when he had grown up, refused to be known as the son of Pharaoh's daughter. He chose to be mistreated along with the people of God rather than to enjoy the pleasures of sin for a short time. He regarded disgrace for the sake of Christ as of greater value than the treasures of Egypt, because he was looking ahead to his reward.

Hebrews 11:24–26

God's Words of Life on
PRIORITIES

Whatever was to my profit I now consider loss for the sake of Christ.

Philippians 3:7

Whatever happens, conduct yourselves in a manner worthy of the gospel of Christ.

Philippians 1:27

I consider my life worth nothing to me, if only I may finish the race and complete the task the Lord Jesus has given me—the task of testifying to the gospel of God's grace.

Acts 20:24

Without faith it is impossible to please God, because anyone who comes to him must believe that he exists and that he rewards those who earnestly seek him.

Hebrews 11:6

We fix our eyes not on what is seen, but on what is unseen. For what is seen is temporary, but what is unseen is eternal.

2 Corinthians 4:18

The only thing that counts is faith expressing itself through love.

Galatians 5:6

God's Words of Life on
PRIORITIES

Let us not love with words or tongue but with actions and in truth.

1 John 3:18

If it is possible, as far as it depends on you, live at peace with everyone.

Romans 12:18

Honor the LORD with your wealth, with the firstfruits of all your crops; then your barns will be filled to overflowing.

Proverbs 3:9–10

Because your love is better than life, O LORD, my lips will glorify you.

Psalm 63:3

Devotional Thought on
PRIORITIES

NUMBER ONE

Sometimes people get so obsessed with something they like—an object, a sport, a famous person or whatever—that they just don't leave time for God. For example, a guy in my small group at church told us he was so into skateboarding that his relationship with God was slipping. He realized he had to change some of his priorities. That got me thinking about my own favorite activities, and I realized I had to make some changes too.

People today have a choice of who or what is number one in their lives. But there's only one right choice: God. If we seek God first, everything else will fall into place the way God wants it to. And while those other things come and go, God will never let us down.

God makes it very clear that we should live our lives for him, above anything or anyone else. Joshua put God first in his life (Joshua 24:15). Have you?

CARISSA

God's Words of Life on
RULES

May the LORD give you discretion and understanding ... so that you may keep the law of the LORD your God. Then you will have success if you are careful to observe the decrees and laws that the LORD gave Moses.

1 Chronicles 22:12–13

We know that we have come to know God if we obey his commands.

1 John 2:3

I run in the path of your commands,
    for you have set my heart free.

Psalm 119:32

Jesus said, "Why do you call me, 'Lord, Lord,' and do not do what I say?"

Luke 6:46

Jesus said, "If you obey my commands, you will remain in my love, just as I have obeyed my Father's commands and remain in his love."

John 15:10

We instructed you how to live in order to please God, as in fact you are living. Now we ask you and urge you in the Lord Jesus to do this more and more.

1 Thessalonians 4:1

God's Words of Life on
RULES

Jesus became the source of eternal salvation
for all who obey him.

Hebrews 5:9

This is love for God: to obey his commands.
And his commands are not burdensome.

1 John 5:3

I have taught you decrees and laws as the LORD
my God commanded me, so that you may follow them in the land you are entering to take
possession of it. Observe them carefully, for
this will show your wisdom and understanding
to the nations.

Deuteronomy 4:5–6

Acknowledge and take to heart this day that
the LORD is God in heaven above and on the
earth below. There is no other. Keep his decrees
and commands, which I am giving you today,
so that it may go well with you.

Deuteronomy 4:39–40

The precepts of the LORD are right,
   giving joy to the heart.
The commands of the LORD are radiant,
   giving light to the eyes.

Psalm 19:8

God's Words of Life on
RULES

Praise the LORD.
Blessed is the man who fears the LORD,
 who finds great delight in his commands.

Psalm 112:1

This is love: that we walk in obedience to God's commands. As you have heard from the beginning, his command is that you walk in love.

2 John 1:6

Children, obey your parents in the Lord, for this is right. "Honor your father and mother"—which is the first commandment with a promise—"that it may go well with you and that you may enjoy long life on the earth."

Ephesians 6:1–3

I will always obey your law,
 for ever and ever.

Psalm 119:44

Devotional Thought on
RULES

GOD'S RULES

By giving us the Ten Commandments, God lets us know that he isn't just some guy who sits back and says, "As long as you say you believe in me, you can do whatever you want." If we go against one of his absolute truths, it's definitely not OK with him.

What's really great about God's rules is that they make sense. We don't just have to follow them because he says so, even though that would be a good enough reason. Following the Ten Commandments makes our lives better too.

Like the one about honoring your parents. Life at home is a lot nicer when you obey Mom and Dad, isn't it? Or the commandment about coveting. Coveting just makes you want more and more but you're never satisfied. If you follow God's rules, you don't have to feel that way.

God really does know what's best for us. Obeying his commandments might seem frustrating sometimes, but it'll make us a lot happier in the end.

KATE

God's Words of Life on
SELF-CONTROL

Surely you desire truth in the inner parts;
   you teach me wisdom in the inmost place.

Psalm 51:6

Since, then, you have been raised with Christ,
set your hearts on things above, where Christ is
seated at the right hand of God. Set your
minds on things above, not on earthly things.

Colossians 3:1–2

Ask where the good way is, and walk in it, and
you will find rest for your souls.

Jeremiah 6:16

Do your best to present yourself to God as one
approved, a workman who does not need to be
ashamed.

2 Timothy 2:15

He who began a good work in you will carry it
on to completion until the day of Christ Jesus.

Philippians 1:6

This is my prayer: that your love may abound
more and more in knowledge and depth of
insight, so that you may be able to discern
what is best and may be pure and blameless
until the day of Christ.

Philippians 1:9–10

God's Words of Life on
SELF•CONTROL

I will set before my eyes
    no vile thing.
The deeds of faithless men I hate;
    they will not cling to me.
Men of perverse heart shall be far from me;
    I will have nothing to do with evil.

Psalm 101:3–4

He who walks righteously and speaks what is
right ... and shuts his eyes against contem-
plating evil—this is the man who will dwell on
the heights.

Isaiah 33:15–16

The mind controlled by the Spirit is life and
peace.

Romans 8:6

The fruit of righteousness will be peace; the
effect of righteousness will be quietness and
confidence forever.

Isaiah 32:17

Jesus said, "Remain in me, and I will remain in
you. No branch can bear fruit by itself; it must
remain in the vine. Neither can you bear fruit
unless you remain in me. I am the vine; you
are the branches. If a man remains in me and I
in him, he will bear much fruit; apart from me
you can do nothing."

John 15:4–5

God's Words of Life on
SELF•CONTROL

Jesus replied, "If anyone loves me, he will obey my teaching. My Father will love him, and we will come to him and make our home with him."

John 14:23

One thing I do: Forgetting what is behind and straining toward what is ahead, I press on toward the goal to win the prize for which God has called me heavenward in Christ Jesus.

Philippians 3:13–14

The grace of God that brings salvation has appeared to all men. It teaches us to say "No" to ungodliness and worldly passions, and to live self-controlled, upright and godly lives in this present age.

Titus 2:11–12

Keep oneself from being polluted by the world.

James 1:27

But the fruit of the Spirit is love, joy, peace, patience, kindness, goodness, faithfulness, gentleness and self-control. Against such things there is no law.

Galatians 5:22–23

Devotional Thought on
SELF•CONTROL

CONTROLLED LIKE CHRIST

When I have a ton of homework, I often get really stressed out and discouraged. It takes all the self-control I have to sit down and actually do my work.

Some of my friends struggle with self-control too. They might give in to temptation and do things they shouldn't, or they might get mad at another person and lose their temper. All of us need to practice self-control and not give in to "evil desires."

Jesus was a great example of how we are supposed to live. He was calm and forgiving. He did the things he needed to do, even when he might have wanted to do something else. Like when he was twelve and he had to leave the temple and go home with his parents. Jesus always made good decisions. When we work at having self-control, we can be more like Jesus.

LISA

God's Words of Life on
SELF•IMAGE

O LORD, you have searched me
    and you know me.
You know when I sit and when I rise;
    you perceive my thoughts from afar.
You discern my going out and my lying down;
    you are familiar with all my ways.
 Before a word is on my tongue
    you know it completely, O LORD.
You hem me in—behind and before;
    you have laid your hand upon me.
Such knowledge is too wonderful for me,
    too lofty for me to attain.
Where can I go from your Spirit?
    Where can I flee from your presence?
If I go up to the heavens, you are there;
    if I make my bed in the depths, you are there.
If I rise on the wings of the dawn,
    if I settle on the far side of the sea,
even there your hand will guide me,
    your right hand will hold me fast. . . .
My frame was not hidden from you
    when I was made in the secret place.
When I was woven together in the depths of
      the earth,
    your eyes saw my unformed body.
All the days ordained for me
    were written in your book
    before one of them came to be.
How precious to me are your thoughts, O God!
    How vast is the sum of them!

Psalm 139:1–10, 15–17

God's Words of Life on
SELF•IMAGE

Then God said, "Let us make man in our image, in our likeness, and let them rule over the fish of the sea and the birds of the air, over the livestock, over all the earth, and over all the creatures that move along the ground." So God created man in his own image, in the image of God he created him; male and female he created them.

Genesis 1:26–27

You created my inmost being;
  you knit me together in my mother's womb.
I praise you because I am fearfully and wonderfully made;
  your works are wonderful, I know that full well.

Psalm 139:13–14

The Lord says, "Before I formed you in the womb I knew you, before you were born I set you apart."

Jeremiah 1:5

Do you not know that your body is a temple of the Holy Spirit, who is in you, whom you have received from God? You are not your own; you were bought at a price. Therefore honor God with your body.

1 Corinthians 6:19–20

God's Words of Life on
SELF-IMAGE

Jesus said, "Are not two sparrows sold for a penny? Yet not one of them will fall to the ground apart from the will of your Father. And even the very hairs of your head are all numbered. So don't be afraid; you are worth more than many sparrows."

Matthew 10:29–31

We are God's workmanship, created in Christ Jesus to do good works, which God prepared in advance for us to do.

Ephesians 2:10

Your beauty should not come from outward adornment, such as braided hair and the wearing of gold jewelry and fine clothes. Instead, it should be that of your inner self, the unfading beauty of a gentle and quiet spirit, which is of great worth in God's sight.

1 Peter 3:3–4

This is what the LORD says—he who created you ... he who formed you ... "Fear not, for I have redeemed you; I have summoned you by name; you are mine."

Isaiah 43:1

Devotional Thought on
SELF•IMAGE

A SPECIAL CREATION

Your body's changing like a Transformer. Your emotions sometimes feel like a never-ending roller coaster. Your relationship with your parents is probably straining and stressing. And your faith, your beliefs about God and Christianity, probably feels like it's been tossed into a microwave—getting zapped and cooked and bombarded with things you don't understand.

Sometimes all this change, all this topsy-turvy confusion, can make you ask questions about yourself. Lots of teens really struggle with their self-image (how you think and feel about yourself). God wants you to understand:

You are a perfect and special creation of God. God made lots and lots of stuff. But he tells you in the Bible that you are his best work and the most favorite thing he created.

God knows everything about you and loves you exactly the way you are. Even more than you know about yourself. Even with all the changes you're going through!

You are a child of God! If you've started a relationship with God, he says you are his kid! Knowing that you're a child of the God of the universe should help your self-image a bit, don't you think?

God's Words of Life on
SEX

Let your eyes look straight ahead, fix your gaze directly before you. Make level paths for your feet and take only ways that are firm. Do not swerve to the right or the left; keep your foot from evil.

Proverbs 4:25–27

It is God's will that you should be sanctified: that you should avoid sexual immorality; that each of you should learn to control his own body in a way that is holy and honorable, … and that in this matter no one should wrong his brother or take advantage of him. … For God did not call us to be impure, but to live a holy life.

1 Thessalonians 4:3–4, 6–7

Do not arouse or awaken love until it so desires.

Song of Songs 2:7

You were bought at a price. Therefore honor God with your body.

1 Corinthians 6:20

The world and its desires pass away, but the man who does the will of God lives forever.

1 John 2:17

The body is not meant for sexual immorality, but for the Lord, and the Lord for the body.

1 Corinthians 6:13

God's Words of Life on
SEX

When you are tempted, God will also provide a way out so that you can stand up under it.

1 Corinthians 10:13

May God himself, the God of peace, sanctify you through and through. May your whole spirit, soul and body be kept blameless at the coming of our Lord Jesus Christ. The one who calls you is faithful and he will do it.

1 Thessalonians 5:23–24

I desire to do your will, O my God;
    your law is within my heart.

Psalm 40:8

Pursue righteousness, faith, love and peace, along with those who call on the Lord out of a pure heart.

2 Timothy 2:22

Live as children of light (for the fruit of the light consists in all goodness, righteousness and truth) and find out what pleases the Lord.

Ephesians 5:8–10

Treat younger men as brothers ... and younger women as sisters, with absolute purity.

1 Timothy 5:1–2

God's Words of Life on
SEX

Be devoted to one another in brotherly love. Honor one another above yourselves.

Romans 12:10

Love is patient, love is kind. It does not envy, it does not boast, it is not proud. It is not rude, it is not self-seeking, it is not easily angered, it keeps no record of wrongs. Love does not delight in evil but rejoices with the truth. It always protects, always trusts, always hopes, always perseveres. Love never fails.

1 Corinthians 13:4–8

Encourage one another and build each other up.

1 Thessalonians 5:11

Show proper respect to everyone.

1 Peter 2:17

Devotional Thought on
SEX

LIVING ON THE EDGE

Imagine looking through a store window at something you really want. But the store is closed. Would you break the window and steal it? Of course not!

No one in their right mind would go for that! But it's kind of like that with sexual temptation. If you give in, you might be happy for a few minutes, or even a few days, but in the end there are real consequences. The guilt starts to set in. So does the regret.

I never like to think about those. Satan does a good job of tricking us when it comes to sexual temptation. Often, he blinds us so we can't even see the danger. All of us need the wisdom of God and the voice of the Holy Spirit to help us avoid this dangerous trap.

I can't play with fire for very long without getting burned. Sooner or later, the consequences of sin will catch up with me. When I think of it that way, it isn't hard to say no.

God's Words of Life on
STRESS

In the day of my trouble I will call to you, Lord,
for you will answer me.

Psalm 86:7

Cast your cares on the LORD
and he will sustain you;
he will never let the righteous fall.

Psalm 55:22

Praise be to the Lord, to God our Savior, who
daily bears our burdens.

Psalm 68:19

When you pass through the waters, I will be
with you; and when you pass through the
rivers, they will not sweep over you. When you
walk through the fire, you will not be burned;
the flames will not set you ablaze. For I am the
LORD, your God.

Isaiah 43:2–3

What you decide on will be done, and light
will shine on your ways.

Job 22:28

Humility and the fear of the LORD
bring wealth and honor and life.

Proverbs 22:4

LORD, you establish peace for us; all that we
have accomplished you have done for us.

Isaiah 26:12

God's Words of Life on
STRESS

You will keep in perfect peace him whose mind is steadfast, because he trusts in you. Trust in the LORD forever, for the LORD, the LORD, is the Rock eternal.

Isaiah 26:3–4

May the Lord of peace himself give you peace at all times and in every way. The Lord be with all of you.

2 Thessalonians 3:16

I will listen to what God the LORD will say;
    he promises peace to his people.

Psalm 85:8

Great peace have they who love your law,
    and nothing can make them stumble.

Psalm 119:165

Since we have been justified through faith, we have peace with God through our Lord Jesus Christ, through whom we have gained access by faith into this grace in which we now stand. And we rejoice in the hope of the glory of God.

Romans 5:1–2

Let the peace of Christ rule in your hearts, since as members of one body you were called to peace. And be thankful.

Colossians 3:15

God's Words of Life on
STRESS

Jesus said, "Come to me, all you who are weary and burdened, and I will give you rest. Take my yoke upon you and learn from me, for I am gentle and humble in heart, and you will find rest for your souls. For my yoke is easy and my burden is light."

Matthew 11:28–30

This is what the Sovereign LORD, the Holy One of Israel, says: "In repentance and rest is your salvation, in quietness and trust is your strength."

Isaiah 30:15

Because so many people were coming and going that [the disciples] did not even have a chance to eat, Jesus said to them, "Come with me by yourselves to a quiet place and get some rest."

Mark 6:31

"I will refresh the weary and satisfy the faint," says the LORD.

Jeremiah 31:25

By the seventh day God had finished the work he had been doing; so on the seventh day he rested from all his work.

Genesis 2:2

There remains, then, a Sabbath-rest for the people of God; for anyone who enters God's rest also rests from his own work, just as God did from his.

Hebrews 4:9–10

Devotional Thought on
STRESS

GET A GRIP ON STRESS

I don't handle stress well. When I was in seventh grade, I got behind on my school-work. I got super worried about missing due dates and turning reports in late. I was too stressed out to concentrate, so the work just piled up. I couldn't sleep very well, I felt sort of sick all the time, and I even got into fights with my friends.

I finally figured out I needed God's help to deal with all my stress. And sure enough, God helped me calm down and get a grip on my life again. No matter how stressful my life gets, I know I can handle it with God's help.

When you feel stressed out, make a list of what's on your mind. Then write down what you can do about those things. Take care of the stuff you can control, and don't worry about the stuff you can't.

BRIAN

God's Words of Life on
SWEARING

The tongue of the wise commends knowledge, but the mouth of the fool gushes folly.

Proverbs 15:2

Jesus said, "I tell you that men will have to give account on the day of judgment for every careless word they have spoken. For by your words you will be acquitted, and by your words you will be condemned."

Matthew 12:36–37

You shall not misuse the name of the LORD your God, for the LORD will not hold anyone guiltless who misuses his name.

Exodus 20:7

If anyone curses his God, he will be held responsible.

Leviticus 24:15

Nor should there be obscenity, foolish talk or coarse joking, which are out of place, but rather thanksgiving.

Ephesians 5:4

Do not let any unwholesome talk come out of your mouths but only what is helpful for building others up according to their needs, that it may benefit those who listen.

Ephesians 4:29

Devotional Thought on
SWEARING

CHOOSING YOUR WORDS

You wouldn't believe the number of kids at my school who lie, swear and say awful things to each other. When you walk down the hall, you can always hear people swearing and can see them getting into fights. It really bugs me!

One time, some kids came up to the boy whose locker is next to mine and started shouting at him, swearing at him and shoving him. Finally I said, "Hey guys, cut it out!" They just laughed at me and kept swearing and yelling. But before long, they stopped and walked away.

Whenever we hear people swearing or see them acting mean, we should not be afraid to tell them to stop. Most people, even if they're not Christians, know it's not right to abuse or swear at people. When we confront them, they might think, *You know, maybe it's not so cool to talk this way.* They might laugh at us, but we'll still be letting them know that not everyone appreciates violence or bad language.

We need to try to be kind and fair in the things we say. That's something no one can argue with.

LAURA

God's Words of Life on
SPIRITUAL GROWTH

Jesus said, "Remain in me, and I will remain in you. No branch can bear fruit by itself; it must remain in the vine. Neither can you bear fruit unless you remain in me. I am the vine; you are the branches. If a man remains in me and I in him, he will bear much fruit; apart from me you can do nothing . . . . If you remain in me and my words remain in you, ask whatever you wish, and it will be given you. This is to my Father's glory, that you bear much fruit, showing yourselves to be my disciples.

John 15:4–5, 7–8

Whoever lives by the truth comes into the light, so that it may be seen plainly that what he has done has been done through God.

John 3:21

The one who sows to please the Spirit, from the Spirit will reap eternal life.

Galatians 6:8

Forgetting what is behind and straining toward what is ahead, I press on toward the goal to win the prize for which God has called me heavenward in Christ Jesus.

Philippians 3:13–14

Jesus said, "Whoever believes in me, as the Scripture has said, streams of living water will flow from within him."

John 7:38

God's Words of Life on
SPIRITUAL GROWTH

Grow in the grace and knowledge of our Lord and Savior Jesus Christ. To him be glory both now and forever!

2 Peter 3:18

Dear friends, build yourselves up in your most holy faith and pray in the Holy Spirit. Keep yourselves in God's love as you wait for the mercy of our Lord Jesus Christ to bring you to eternal life.... To him who is able to keep you from falling and to present you before his glorious presence without fault and with great joy—to the only God our Savior be glory, majesty, power and authority, through Jesus Christ our Lord, before all ages, now and forevermore! Amen.

Jude 20–21, 24–25

We have not stopped praying for you and asking God to fill you with the knowledge of his will through all spiritual wisdom and understanding. And we pray this in order that you may live a life worthy of the Lord and may please him in every way: bearing fruit in every good work, growing in the knowledge of God.

Colossians 1:9–10

Teach me knowledge and good judgment,
for I believe in your commands.

Psalm 119:66

God's Words of Life on
SPIRITUAL GROWTH

It was God who gave some to be ... pastors and teachers, to prepare God's people for works of service, so that the body of Christ may be built up until we all reach unity in the faith and in the knowledge of the Son of God and become mature, attaining to the whole measure of the fullness of Christ. Then we will no longer be infants, tossed back and forth by the waves, and blown here and there by every wind of teaching ... Instead, speaking the truth in love, we will in all things grow up into him who is the Head, that is, Christ. From him the whole body, joined and held together by every supporting ligament, grows and builds itself up in love, as each part does its work.

Ephesians 4:11–16

Like newborn babies, crave pure spiritual milk, so that by it you may grow up in your salvation, now that you have tasted that the Lord is good.

1 Peter 2:2–3

Apply your heart to instruction
   and your ears to words of knowledge.

Proverbs 23:12

Devotional Thought on
SPIRITUAL GROWTH

YOUR OWN FAITH

Faith is not only *what* you believe, but also *how* you live. Here you are, growing up, believing in God, the God your parents hopefully told you about, the God your youth worker tells you about, and now you are beginning to wonder who this God really is and how true is this God. In other words, you are beginning the process of making faith your own.

So how do you make your faith your own?

First. Discover what faith is by learning from your mistakes. Look at the disciples. They constantly made mistakes; but in the process they learned what their faith was and what it wasn't.

Second. Faith sometimes comes when we just stop doing stuff and think about life. Thinking is a great way to figure out faith and life.

Third. It's amazing what we can learn about faith when we watch others who have faith.

Fourth. Take a risk! Share your faith with your friends, stand up for what you believe!

Fifth. Talk about it. The more you talk about your faith, the more it becomes your own.

God's Words of Life on
TEMPTATION

Because Jesus himself suffered when he was tempted, he is able to help those who are being tempted.

Hebrews 2:18

You know that he appeared so that he might take away our sins. And in him is no sin. No one who lives in him keeps on sinning. No one who continues to sin has either seen him or known him.

1 John 3:5-6

I acknowledged my sin to you
    and did not cover up my iniquity.
I said, "I will confess
    my transgressions to the LORD"—
and you forgave
    the guilt of my sin.

Psalm 32:5

He who conceals his sins does not prosper.

Proverbs 28:13

All of us also lived among them at one time, gratifying the cravings of our sinful nature and following its desires and thoughts. Like the rest, we were by nature objects of wrath. But because of his great love for us, God, who is rich in mercy, made us alive with Christ even when we were dead in transgressions—it is by grace you have been saved.

Ephesians 2:3-5

God's Words of Life on
TEMPTATION

God is faithful; he will not let you be tempted beyond what you can bear. But when you are tempted, he will also provide a way out so that you can stand up under it.

1 Corinthians 10:13

Forgive us our sins, for we also forgive everyone who sins against us. And lead us not into temptation.

Luke 11:4

Our struggle is not against flesh and blood, but against the rulers, against the authorities, against the powers of this dark world and against the spiritual forces of evil in the heavenly realms.

Ephesians 6:12

God has delivered us from such a deadly peril, and he will deliver us. On him we have set our hope that he will continue to deliver us.

2 Corinthians 1:10

The Lord will rescue me from every evil attack and will bring me safely to his heavenly kingdom. To him be glory for ever and ever.

2 Timothy 4:18

Watch and pray so that you will not fall into temptation. The spirit is willing, but the body is weak.

Matthew 26:41

God's Words of Life on
TEMPTATION

We know that our old self was crucified with him so that the body of sin might be done away with, that we should no longer be slaves to sin.

Romans 6:6

Do not offer the parts of your body to sin, as instruments of wickedness, but rather offer yourselves to God, as those who have been brought from death to life; and offer the parts of your body to him as instruments of right-eousness.

Romans 6:13

Since we are surrounded by such a great cloud of witnesses, let us throw off everything that hinders and the sin that so easily entangles and let us run with perseverance the race marked out for us.

Hebrews 12:1

Devotional Thought on
TEMPTATION

SHOULD I STAY OR GO?

Is it just me, or is junior high one temptation after another? Like the party I was invited to a while ago. The person having the party invited 12 guys and girls, enough to make 6 couples. And even though the person said it wasn't going to be a make-out party and that their parents would be around, I still knew there'd be a lot of temptation to pair off with some girl and make out. That's why I decided not to go.

I don't know what would have happened if I'd been at that party. Maybe everything would have been fine and I would've just had fun with my friends. But since I wasn't sure, I stayed away.

If you ask me, God's a no-nonsense God. He's pretty clear about how he wants us to live He wants us to seek good and stay away from evil, period. It's not always easy, but it's what's right.

MIKE

God's Words of Life on
THANKFULNESS

Praise the LORD.
Give thanks to the LORD, for he is good;
    his love endures forever.

Psalm 106:1

I will extol the LORD at all times;
    his praise will always be on my lips.

Psalm 34:1

Give thanks in all circumstances, for this is
God's will for you in Christ Jesus.

1 Thessalonians 5:18

Thanks be to God! He gives us the victory
through our Lord Jesus Christ.

1 Corinthians 15:57

Thanks be to God for his indescribable gift!

2 Corinthians 9:15

Give thanks to the LORD, call on his name; make
known among the nations what he has done.

1 Chronicles 16:8

Praise the LORD.
I will extol the LORD with all my heart
    in the council of the upright and in the
        assembly.
Great are the works of the LORD;
    they are pondered by all who delight in them.

Psalm 111:1–2

God's Words of Life on
THANKFULNESS

Sing to the LORD with thanksgiving;
    make music to our God on the harp.

Psalm 147:7

Enter his gates with thanksgiving
    and his courts with praise;
give thanks to him and praise his name.

Psalm 100:4

I will sacrifice a thank offering to you
    and call on the name of the LORD.

Psalm 116:17

Give thanks to the LORD, call on his name;
    make known among the nations what he
        has done,
    and proclaim that his name is exalted.
Sing to the LORD, for he has done glorious
        things;
    let this be known to all the world.

Isaiah 12:4–5

Whatever you do, whether in word or deed, do
it all in the name of the Lord Jesus, giving
thanks to God the Father through him.

Colossians 3:17

The LORD is my strength and my shield;
    my heart trusts in him, and I am helped.
My heart leaps for joy
    and I will give thanks to him in song.

Psalm 28:7

God's Words of Life on
THANKFULNESS

We give thanks to you, Lord God Almighty, the One who is and who was, because you have taken your great power and have begun to reign.

Revelation 11:17

I thank Christ Jesus our Lord, who has given me strength.

1 Timothy 1:12

Let the peace of Christ rule in your hearts, since as members of one body you were called to peace. And be thankful.

Colossians 3:15

I always thank my God as I remember you in my prayers, because I hear about your faith in the Lord Jesus and your love for all the saints.

Philemon 4–5

Everything God created is good, and nothing is to be rejected if it is received with thanksgiving, because it is consecrated by the word of God and prayer.

1 Timothy 4:4–5

Devotional Thought on
THANKFULNESS

GIVE THANKS

Even if your life's pretty tough, you still have a lot to be thankful for. A bunch of reasons to be thankful: God's love and protection; God's provision for us; forgiveness from God and others; and being able to share with others.

When you read Psalm 100, it's totally obvious that the writer is joyful and thankful! Look at verse 4: "Enter his gates with thanksgiving and his courts with praise; give thanks to him and praise his name." It mentions giving thanks twice; and it mentions the word *praise* twice! Sometimes the word *praise* can sound like a real "churchy" word, and you might wonder what it means to praise God. It's simple: We praise God by giving thanks to him and telling him how much we appreciate all the things he's done for us! More importantly we thank and praise him simply for who he is: our super-loving, perfect Dad!

God's Words of Life on
TROUBLE

Jesus said, "In this world you will have trouble. But take heart! I have overcome the world."

John 16:33

Endure hardship with us like a good soldier of Christ Jesus.

2 Timothy 2:3

It has been granted to you on behalf of Christ not only to believe on him, but also to suffer for him.

Philippians 1:29

He was despised and rejected by men, a man of sorrows, and familiar with suffering.

Isaiah 53:3

Just as the sufferings of Christ flow over into our lives, so also through Christ our comfort overflows.

2 Corinthians 1:5

Our present sufferings are not worth comparing with the glory that will be revealed in us.

Romans 8:18

He knows the way that I take; when he has tested me, I will come forth as gold.

Job 23:10

God's Words of Life on
TROUBLE

The LORD disciplines those he loves.

Proverbs 3:12

If you are insulted because of the name of Christ, you are blessed, for the Spirit of glory and of God rests on you.

1 Peter 4:14

Everyone who wants to live a godly life in Christ Jesus will be persecuted.

2 Timothy 3:12

We also rejoice in our sufferings, because we know that suffering produces perseverance; perseverance, character; and character, hope.

Romans 5:3–4

Consider it pure joy ... whenever you face trials of many kinds, because you know that the testing of your faith develops perseverance.

James 1:2–3

He has not despised or disdained
　　the suffering of the afflicted one;
he has not hidden his face from him
　　but has listened to his cry for help.

Psalm 22:24

The LORD is a refuge for the oppressed,
　　a stronghold in times of trouble.

Psalm 9:9

God's Words of Life on
TROUBLE

You will surely forget your trouble,
    recalling it only as waters gone by.
Life will be brighter than noonday,
    and darkness will become like morning.
You will be secure, because there is hope;
      you will look about you and take your rest
        in safety.

Job 11:16–18

God is our refuge and strength,
    an ever-present help in trouble.

Psalm 46:1

Praise be to the God and Father of our Lord
Jesus Christ, the Father of compassion and the
God of all comfort, who comforts us in all our
troubles, so that we can comfort those in any
trouble with the comfort we ourselves have
received from God.

2 Corinthians 1:3–4

Devotional Thought on
TROUBLE

STUFF HAPPENS

When tragic things happen, we make a mistake if we blame them on God. The Bible clearly says that God does not create evil. God doesn't make bad things happen. In the midst of bad things, God works to bring good out of it all (Romans 8:28). God is able to take our tragedies, and the mistakes we make, and turn them into something beautiful.

I'm a college professor. Sometimes I ask my students, "What is the most evil thing that ever happened in human history?" They always answer, "The crucifixion of Jesus!" Then I ask, "What is the most wonderful thing that ever happened in human history?" The same students say, "The crucifixion of Jesus!" This horrible event, which was the result of our sin, was taken by God and transformed into something that has blessed people everywhere.

God doesn't make bad things happen, but he is at work in the middle of all things, overcoming evil with good and turning tragedy into blessings. So, instead of asking, "Why does God allow bad things to happen?" we should be asking, "What can God do through this tragedy? How can I work with God to turn this into something good?"

TONY CAMPOLO

God's Words of Life on
WISDOM

If any of you lacks wisdom, he should ask God, who gives generously to all without finding fault, and it will be given to him.

James 1:5

The fear of the Lord—that is wisdom, and to shun evil is understanding.

Job 28:28

Jesus said, "Everyone who hears these words of mine and puts them into practice is like a wise man who built his house on the rock. The rain came down, the streams rose, and the winds blew and beat against that house; yet it did not fall, because it had its foundation on the rock. But everyone who hears these words of mine and does not put them into practice is like a foolish man who built his house on sand. The rain came down, the streams rose, and the winds blew and beat against that house, and it fell with a great crash."

Matthew 7:24–27

Get wisdom, get understanding; do not forget my words or swerve from them. Do not forsake wisdom, and she will protect you; love her, and she will watch over you. Wisdom is supreme; therefore get wisdom. Though it cost all you have, get understanding.

Proverbs 4:5–7

God's Words of Life on
WISDOM

Whether you turn to the right or to the left, your ears will hear a voice behind you, saying, "This is the way; walk in it."

Isaiah 30:21

The wisdom that comes from heaven is first of all pure; then peace-loving, considerate, submissive, full of mercy and good fruit, impartial and sincere.

James 3:17

If you accept my words and store up my commands within you, turning your ear to wisdom and applying your heart to understanding, and if you call out for insight and cry aloud for understanding, and if you look for it as for silver and search for it as for hidden treasure, then you will understand the fear of the LORD and find the knowledge of God. For the LORD gives wisdom, and from his mouth come knowledge and understanding.

Proverbs 2:1–6

Where then does wisdom come from? Where does understanding dwell? It is hidden from the eyes of every living thing, concealed even from the birds of the air ... God understands the way to it and he alone knows where it dwells.

Job 28:20–21, 23

God's Words of Life on
WISDOM

The foolishness of God is wiser than man's wisdom, and the weakness of God is stronger than man's strength.

1 Corinthians 1:25

I guide you in the way of wisdom and lead you along straight paths. When you walk, your steps will not be hampered; when you run, you will not stumble.

Proverbs 4:11–12

Pay attention to my wisdom, listen well to my words of insight, that you may maintain discretion and your lips may preserve knowledge.

Proverbs 5:1–2

Whoever listens to me will live in safety and be at ease, without fear of harm.

Proverbs 1:33

I thought, 'Age should speak;
    advanced years should teach wisdom.'
But it is the spirit in a man,
    the breath of the Almighty, that gives him
        understanding.
It is not only the old who are wise,
    not only the aged who understand what is
        right.

Job 32:7–9

Devotional Thought on
WISDOM

JUST WHAT WE NEED

If God ever came to me and said I could have anything I wanted, I sure hope I'd ask for wisdom like Solomon did. I mean, think about what Solomon did here. He could have had *anything*—all the money and fame in the world, power over all his enemies—anything at all. And what did he choose? Wisdom.

Of all the things Solomon might have wanted, the thing he wanted most was the wisdom to do God's will. He wanted to be a good king who would follow God and make good decisions. God gave Solomon just what he asked for and a lot more: God made Solomon the wisest man who ever lived, plus one of the richest and most honored.

All of us could use a little more wisdom. Most people have a hard time making good decisions, and a lot of Christians struggle to follow God. When we ask God to help us grow closer to him and live for him, he'll give us exactly what we need to do it.

BRET

God's Words of Life on
WITNESSING

Jesus came to them and said, "All authority in heaven and on earth has been given to me. Therefore go and make disciples of all nations, baptizing them in the name of the Father and of the Son and of the Holy Spirit, and teaching them to obey everything I have commanded you. And surely I am with you always, to the very end of the age."

Matthew 28:18–20

Jesus said, "I tell you that in the same way there will be more rejoicing in heaven over one sinner who repents than over ninety-nine righteous persons who do not need to repent."

Luke 15:7

If you confess with your mouth, "Jesus is Lord," and believe in your heart that God raised him from the dead, you will be saved. For it is with your heart that you believe and are justified, and it is with your mouth that you confess and are saved.

Romans 10:9–10

Jesus said, "The Spirit of the Lord is on me, because he has anointed me to preach good news to the poor. He has sent me to proclaim freedom for the prisoners and recovery of sight for the blind, to release the oppressed, to proclaim the year of the Lord's favor."

Luke 4:18–19

God's Words of Life on
WITNESSING

Jesus said, "Whoever acknowledges me before men, I will also acknowledge him before my Father in heaven."

Matthew 10:32

Let your light shine before men, that they may see your good deeds and praise your Father in heaven.

Matthew 5:16

Jesus said to them, "Go into all the world and preach the good news to all creation. Whoever believes and is baptized will be saved, but whoever does not believe will be condemned."

Mark 16:15–16

Jesus said, "Anyone who has faith in me will do what I have been doing. He will do even greater things than these, because I am going to the Father."

John 14:12

May I never boast except in the cross of our Lord Jesus Christ, through which the world has been crucified to me, and I to the world.

Galatians 6:14

Those who are wise will shine like the brightness of the heavens, and those who lead many to righteousness, like the stars for ever and ever.

Daniel 12:3

God's Words of Life on
WITNESSING

Jesus said, "You will receive power when the Holy Spirit comes on you; and you will be my witnesses in Jerusalem, and in all Judea and Samaria, and to the ends of the earth."

Acts 1:8

"You are my witnesses," declares the LORD, "and my servant whom I have chosen, so that you may know and believe me and understand that I am he ... I have revealed and saved and proclaimed—I, and not some foreign god among you. You are my witnesses," declares the LORD, "that I am God."

Isaiah 43:10, 12

Now go; I will help you speak and will teach you what to say.

Exodus 4:12

"You must speak my words to them, whether they listen or fail to listen," says the LORD.

Ezekiel 2:7

[The Temple Council] called [Peter and John] in again and commanded them not to speak or teach at all in the name of Jesus. But Peter and John replied, "Judge for yourselves whether it is right in God's sight to obey you rather than God. For we cannot help speaking about what we have seen and heard."

Acts 4:18–20

Devotional Thought on
WITNESSING

I'll Go!

On the last night of our youth retreat, our youth pastor opened the mike up to us and invited us to talk about what God had done in our lives. We all just sat there. I finally went up, hoping God would have something to say through me. As I opened my mouth, I felt God giving me the words to say. I ignored my fears about talking in front of people and found out that I have a gift for sharing God's Word with others. Now I'm a regular speaker at my school's Fellowship of Christian Students.

That experience showed me that anyone willing to say, "Lord, send me" will be sent. Everyone has gifts. And God, the Creator and Ruler of the universe, uses the gifts of ordinary people to do his work. What a privilege!

Be open to God's plans for you and tell him you want to be called. And hang on tight, because when God starts using you, you move fast!

PATRICK

God's Words of Life on
WORK

We continually remember before our God and
Father your work produced by faith, your labor
prompted by love, and your endurance inspired
by hope in our Lord Jesus Christ.

1 Thessalonians 1:3

Always give yourselves fully to the work of the
Lord, because you know that your labor in the
Lord is not in vain.

1 Corinthians 15:58

Six days you shall labor, but on the seventh
day you shall rest.

Exodus 34:21

Jesus said, "I know your deeds, your hard work
and your perseverance. ... You have persevered and have endured hardships for my
name, and have not grown weary."

Revelation 2:2–3

God is not unjust; he will not forget your work
and the love you have shown him as you have
helped his people and continue to help them.
We want each of you to show this same dili-
gence to the very end, in order to make your
hope sure. We do not want you to become lazy,
but to imitate those who through faith and
patience inherit what has been promised.

Hebrews 6:10–12

Whatever you do, work at it with all your heart, as working for the Lord, not for men, since you know that you will receive an inheritance from the Lord as a reward.

Colossians 3:23–24

God is able to make all grace abound to you, so that in all things at all times, having all that you need, you will abound in every good work.

2 Corinthians 9:8

When God gives any man wealth and possessions, and enables him to enjoy them, to accept his lot and be happy in his work—this is a gift of God.

Ecclesiastes 5:19

Whatever your hand finds to do, do it with all your might.

Ecclesiastes 9:10

All hard work brings a profit.

Proverbs 14:23

May the favor of the Lord our God rest upon us; establish the work of our hands for us.

Psalm 90:17

Be strong and do not give up, for your work will be rewarded.

2 Chronicles 15:7

God's Words of Life on
WORK

The LORD will open the heavens, the storehouse of his bounty, to send rain on your land in season and to bless all the work of your hands.

Deuteronomy 28:12

Don't let anyone look down on you because you are young, but set an example for the believers in speech, in life, in love, in faith and in purity. Until I come, devote yourself to the public reading of Scripture, to preaching and to teaching. Do not neglect your gift ...
Be diligent in these matters; give yourself wholly to them, so that everyone may see your progress.

1 Timothy 4:12–15

May the Lord direct your hearts into God's love and Christ's perseverance.

2 Thessalonians 3:5

I can do everything through Christ who gives me strength.

Philippians 4:13

Devotional Thought on
WORK

A TIME FOR EVERYTHING

God gives us work to do on earth. Most of the time, just knowing God doesn't automatically make the work easy. We'll have many difficulties. God will provide for our needs, though, and we need to accept the work he has for us—even if it's hard.

Ecclesiastes 3:1–11 is a great passage to remember when you're having a hard time. It reminds us that there is a time for everything. Life won't always be easy and perfect, but that doesn't mean God has lost control. He has special work cut out for each of us as Christians. He can see the whole picture, so he knows how the good and bad will fit together in the end. We just need to obey him, do his work and trust him *always*!

BECCA

God's Words of Life on
WORRY

Trust in him and he will do this:
> He will make your righteousness shine like
>   the dawn,
the justice of your cause like the noonday sun.

Psalm 37:5–6

Do not be anxious about anything, but in
everything, by prayer and petition, with
thanksgiving, present your requests to God.
And the peace of God, which transcends all
understanding, will guard your hearts and your
minds in Christ Jesus.

Philippians 4:6–7

Do not be afraid, little flock, for your Father
has been pleased to give you the kingdom.

Luke 12:32

The LORD himself goes before you and will be
with you; he will never leave you nor forsake
you. Do not be afraid; do not be discouraged.

Deuteronomy 31:8

No one will be able to stand up against you all
the days of your life. As I was with Moses, so I
will be with you; I will never leave you nor
forsake you.

Joshua 1:5

God did not give us a spirit of timidity, but a
spirit of power, of love and of self-discipline.

2 Timothy 1:7

God's Words of Life on
WORRY

Jesus said: "Therefore I tell you, do not worry about your life, what you will eat or drink; or about your body, what you will wear. Is not life more important than food, and the body more important than clothes? Look at the birds of the air; they do not sow or reap or store away in barns, and yet your heavenly Father feeds them. Are you not much more valuable than they? Who of you by worrying can add a single hour to his life?

"And why do you worry about clothes? See how the lilies of the field grow. They do not labor or spin. Yet I tell you that not even Solomon in all his splendor was dressed like one of these. If that is how God clothes the grass of the field, which is here today and tomorrow is thrown into the fire, will he not much more clothe you, O you of little faith? So do not worry, saying, 'What shall we eat?' or 'What shall we drink?' or 'What shall we wear?' For the pagans run after all these things, and your heavenly Father knows that you need them. But seek first his kingdom and his righteousness, and all these things will be given to you as well. Therefore do not worry about tomorrow, for tomorrow will worry about itself. Each day has enough trouble of its own."

Matthew 6:25–34

God's Words of Life on
WORRY

Those who trust in the LORD are like Mount Zion,
which cannot be shaken but endures forever.

Psalm 125:1

Those who know your name will trust in you,
for you, LORD, have never forsaken those
who seek you.

Psalm 9:10

Trust in the LORD with all your heart
and lean not on your own understanding;
in all your ways acknowledge him,
and he will make your paths straight.

Proverbs 3:5–6

Surely God is my salvation;
I will trust and not be afraid.
The LORD, the LORD, is my strength and my song;
he has become my salvation.

Isaiah 12:2

He who fears the LORD has a secure fortress.

Proverbs 14:26

The LORD blesses his people with peace.

Psalm 29:11

Devotional Thought on
WORRY

NO STRESS TESTS

I tend to get pretty stressed out about tests. But Matthew 6:25–34 tells me not to get so worried about stuff like school. That doesn't mean I should give up studying and just wait for God to help me pass my tests. It just means that as long as God is first in my life, I can be confident that he'll give me everything I need.

I like the way the passage talks about God caring for even the smallest animals. If he looks after them, I know he'll look after me, because God loves me even more than the animals. He'll always take care of me. And when I look at my life, I know that's true. I have friends, a family who cares about me, a place to live, food to eat and clothes to wear.

Seeing the way God takes care of the big things in my life, I know I can trust him to take care of the little things too. So I don't have to stress out about anything, including tests!

JESSICA

God's Words of Life on
WORSHIP

Great is the LORD and most worthy of praise;
  his greatness no one can fathom.

Psalm 145:3

Ascribe to the LORD the glory due his name.
Bring an offering and come before him; worship the LORD in the splendor of his holiness.

1 Chronicles 16:29

Holy, holy, holy is the LORD Almighty; the whole earth is full of his glory.

Isaiah 6:3

I, by your great mercy,
  will come into your house;
in reverence will I bow down.

Psalm 5:7

Whenever the living creatures give glory, honor and thanks to him who sits on the throne and who lives for ever and ever, the twenty-four elders fall down before him who sits on the throne, and worship him who lives for ever and ever. They lay their crowns before the throne and say: "You are worthy, our Lord and God, to receive glory and honor and power, for you created all things, and by your will they were created and have their being."

Revelation 4:9–11

God's Words of Life on
WORSHIP

Come, let us bow down in worship,
    let us kneel before the LORD our Maker;
for he is our God
    and we are the people of his pasture,
the flock under his care.

Psalm 95:6–7

Since we are receiving a kingdom that cannot
be shaken, let us be thankful, and so worship
God acceptably with reverence and awe.

Hebrews 12:28

Ascribe to the LORD the glory due his name;
    worship the LORD in the splendor of his
        holiness.

Psalm 29:2

The LORD is my strength and my song; he has
become my salvation. He is my God, and I
will praise him, my father's God, and I will
exalt him.

Exodus 15:2

A time is coming and has now come when the
true worshipers will worship the Father in
spirit and truth, for they are the kind of worshipers the Father seeks. God is spirit, and his
worshipers must worship in spirit and in truth.

John 4:23–24

God's Words of Life on
WORSHIP

Worship the LORD with gladness;
    come before him with joyful songs.

Psalm 100:2

I will praise you, O LORD, with all my heart;
    I will tell of all your wonders.
I will be glad and rejoice in you;
    I will sing praise to your name, O Most High.

Psalm 9:1–2

Praise be to the God and Father of our Lord
Jesus Christ, who has blessed us in the heavenly
realms with every spiritual blessing in Christ.

Ephesians 1:3

I will praise you forever for what you have done;
    in your name I will hope, for your name is
       good.
I will praise you in the presence of your saints.

Psalm 52:9

The LORD lives! Praise be to my Rock!
    Exalted be God, the Rock, my Savior!

2 Samuel 22:47

Praise be to the God and Father of our Lord
Jesus Christ! In his great mercy he has given us
new birth into a living hope through the resurrection of Jesus Christ from the dead.

1 Peter 1:3

Devotional Thought on
WORSHIP

WORSHIP WITH YOUR HEART

It would be weird to go to a roller rink and not skate. Or to go to a game and not cheer. Or to go to church and not sing. We've got to get into worship, heart and soul.

But why is it so important? What happens when we worship?

First, *God* feels good. He loves nothing better than to hear his kids belt out his praises. Your worship brings a huge smile to his face.

Second, *believers* grow through worship. They get in touch with God; they sing words that strengthen their faith.

Third, *outsiders* are drawn to God when we worship. They see our love and start wondering, "What's up with these people? They actually believe God is here!" That's the first step in reaching them.

Fourth, *enemies* are defeated. That's the point of the story in 2 Chronicles 20. When God's people faced a huge army, they marched to the battle lines singing. They knew they couldn't win by swinging swords, so they launched worship warheads—and it worked. As they began to sing, the Lord ambushed the invaders and they were defeated! So worship hard—who knows what may happen as a result!

ACKNOWLEDGMENTS

Many youth pastors, youth workers and teens from all over the nation helped provide the devotions for the *Teen Devotional Bible* and this promise book. Some of the contributors not individually mentioned in this book are

DR. CHAP CLARK
GREGG FARAH
SAM FOWLER
CURT GIBSON
RICH GRIFFITH
LAURA GROSS
GREG LAFFERTY
TIM MCLAUGHLIN
MARK OESTREICHER
DARRELL PEARSON
DR. MARV PENNER
KARA ECKMANN POWELL
TODD TEMPLE

ERIC VENABLE
JOHN WILSON
MIKE YACONELLI
FROM *CAMPUS LIFE MAGAZINE*:
CARLA BARNHILL
MARTIN COCKROFT
ELESHA HODGE
DOUG JOHNSON
CHRIS LUTES
MARK MORING
JENNIFER RIDENOUR
MARILYN ROWE